The Church and Women
in the Third World

The Church and Women in the Third World

edited by
John C. B. and Ellen Low Webster

The Westminster Press
Philadelphia

Book design by Gene Harris

First edition

Published by The Westminster Press®
Philadelphia, Pennsylvania

PRINTED IN THE UNITED STATES OF AMERICA

9 8 7 6 5 4 3 2 1

Library of Congress Cataloging in Publication Data

Main entry under title:

The Church and women in the Third World.

  Bibliography: p.
  CONTENTS: Images of Chinese women / Shirley S. Garrett
—Assumptions about the Indian woman underlying Protestant church policies and programs, 1947–1982 / John C. B. Webster
—Catholic women of India / Stella Faria—[etc.]
    1. Women in Christianity—Developing countries—Addresses, essays, lectures. 2. Developing countries—Church history—Addresses, essays, lectures. 3. Women—Developing countries—Social conditions—Addresses, essays, lectures. I. Webster, John C. B., 1935–
II. Webster, Ellen Low.
BV639.W7C48 1985   261.8′344′091724   84-26967
ISBN 0-664-24601-X (pbk.)

To Elizabeth and Marilyn

Contents

III. THE CHURCH AND THE STATUS OF WOMEN

Preface

Although much is being written about Third World churches and Third World women, the scholarly literature linking the two is surprisingly meager. This book is an attempt to fill that void. Fortunately, interest in this subject is growing in both church and academic circles. This book is an attempt to satisfy and increase that interest. It presents some fresh, empirical research—historical and contemporary—along with an annotated bibliography of recent writing on the church and women in Asia, Africa, and Latin America. The more specific concerns underlying the book may best be stated by giving a brief account of its history.

We trace its origins back to a course on "The Church and Women" that we taught together for three years (1979–1981) at United Theological College in Bangalore, India. It was a new course then, as far as we know the first on women to be taught in any Indian theological seminary. Our assumption in teaching it was that critical reflection on both Christian and Indian traditions concerning women was essential to meaningful innovation or change in this important area of the life and mission of Indian churches. Then, in the spring of 1983, we taught a course on "The Church and Women in the Third World" at Pittsburgh Theological Seminary to (mostly) North American students, on the assumption that, if they were to become more global in their stance on women's issues, they would have to understand not only the experience of women who were different from themselves but also the nature and consequences for Third World women of those church ties that have connected North Americans to the Third World.

Both sets of assumptions have been carried over into this book, which is intended to provide a useful resource on what we consider to be an important subject for our own students, for the students of others, and for the church at large. We invited a number of scholars who shared our interest in this subject, but who brought different concerns and competences to it, to contribute essays that would be empirical, rather than theological or prescriptive, on any one or a combination of three themes: Christian images of women, the role of women in the church, and the impact that the church has had on the status of women in general. Those who accepted our invitation have written their essays especially for this book, thus adding to our knowledge of the subject. We thank them not only for being so generous with their time and expertise, but also for their suggestions concerning the book as a whole. We have benefited greatly from getting to know them, or getting to know them better, while working on this project together.

In addition, we thank the staff of the Burke Library of Union Theological Seminary in New York City for their assistance in locating most of the materials for the bibliography, and the staff of the Stony Point Center for their encouragement and hospitality while we were preparing the manuscript.

Stony Point, N.Y.   J. C. B. W.
June 1984   E. L. W.

Introduction

John C. B. Webster

On the fifth day of the World Council of Churches' conference on "The Community of Women and Men in the Church," held at Sheffield, England, in July 1981, the Third World participants told the conference, in effect, that its agenda and discussions did not really take into consideration "who we are" and "where we are coming from." Earlier in the conference Father Tissa Balasuriya, O.M.I., of Sri Lanki had given a plenary address on "Women and Men in New Community: Insights from Liberation Struggles" in which he had stated:

> The priorities of the women's movement are different according to the race, class, or nation to which the women belong. Women of the European and North American continents are mainly concerned with obtaining equal rights with the men within their society. They do not necessarily have objectives of transforming their own social structures or international relations.
>
> On the other hand, for the women of Asia, Africa, and South and Central America their main problems concern the entire social system in which they are involved together with their men. The greater oppression of women in the "Third World" is recognized as related to the ongoing exploitation of the poor countries and races by the rich and powerful nations. These considerations induce the women from the poorer countries to press for a more radical approach to the women's movement. They want the women to give priority to overall social transformation within their countries and in international relations.[1]

It seems that this contrast in perspective had not been given its due until the Third World participants made their brief joint statement. According to one participant, this "cry for recognition was heard and profoundly affected the outcome of the conference."[2]

In their fuller, revised statement, published in the report of the conference, the Third World participants expressed their gratitude "for the awakening of our awareness to sexism in our own churches." "We all," they confessed, "share an experience of being subjugated, controlled, and exploited by men within the larger social context of our countries." They went on to say:

> But when we began to share our experiences as concerned Christians, we were forced to see beyond our noses, because behind those men who dominate with their so-called superiority, we became aware of a faceless, formless beast holding them by their skinny throats, threatening and making objects of us all, women and men. We had to ask what can we do.[3]

In short, they felt that sexism as a barrier to the community of women and men had to be seen and dealt with in a context that was much broader than the church: a societal context that was global in dimension, exploitative and dehumanizing in character, and threatened by nuclear annihilation.

One month later, in New Delhi, India, the Fifth International Conference of the Ecumenical Association of Third World Theologians (EATWOT) had a similar experience when dealing with the theme "Irruption of the Third World: Challenge to Theology." There was an "irruption within the irruption" when one of the women delegates called attention to women's marginalized position within EATWOT, within the theological enterprise, and within the decision-making bodies of the churches.[4] In subsequent reflections, Amba Oduyoye wrote:

> There have been several international meetings at which Third World representatives have said that antisexism is not their priority. . . . The few Third World women who speak that language are just allowing themselves to be co-opted. The fact is that sexism is part of the intricate web of oppression in which most of us live, and that having attuned ourselves to it does not make it any less a factor of oppression. Most Third World women, being literally close to the earth and to the maintenance of their race against classist and racist aggression, have opted to find complete fulfillment in this sacred duty and why not? But that does not mean an approval of sexism. . . . The struggle for a wholesome and life-expanding community of women and men in church and society is bound to be enhanced by viewing feminism in theology as a theology of relationships, and a Third World perspective on it will be a contribution to the global effort. Feminism is anything but the imperialist ploy some would like us to take it for. There may be a lot of red herrings to come, but feminism is certainly not one of them. It is a fact of experience, not a thesis.[5]

She went on to point out that the theological method used within EATWOT was partially to blame for its overlooking feminist perspectives and concerns.

The experiences that have informed the doing of theology in the context of EATWOT have been mainly socio-economic and political and have led largely to the analysis of the roots of classism and racism. The religio-cultural concerns of Africa and Asia and the indigenous peoples of the Americas have been marginal. This I believe has been one of the reasons why sexism, often anchored on religio-cultural perceptions, had not surfaced before.[6]

The final statement of the conference took note of the oppression of women in the Third World, affirmed that without women's perspectives born of experience in their liberational struggles "there can be no truly relevant theology, no genuine social transformation, no holistic human liberation," and committed itself to "supporting women's struggle for equality in and through theology."[7]

Seen from a "Church and Women in the Third World" perspective, these two conferences, held in succeeding months of the same year, stand in beautiful juxtaposition to each other. Each began at a different point to deal with a different agenda and each experienced a different "irruption" that had a direct bearing on the church and women in the Third World. Yet both treated the Third World as a single entity, despite diversities within it; both concluded that the church often does, but should not, separate these two goals—the community of women and men and the liberation of the oppressed. Questions still abound concerning not only how the church is to move from where it is now in various parts of the world toward the interrelated goals of community and liberation but also who is to play what role in the process.

The essays in this book do not seek to answer those questions so much as two prior questions that need more systematic study than they have received so far: What is the present relationship between the church and women in various Third World contexts, and how did it get to be that way? The essays do differ in the kind of subject matter they treat, as well as in the perspectives, data, and methodologies they employ, but all of them are empirical studies of the past or present that examine three facets of the relationship between the church and women: Christian images of women, the role of women in the church, and the church's role in affecting the status of women.

It may be premature to draw conclusions about the present relationship of the church and women in the Asian, African, and Latin-American contexts, as well as about how and why those relationships came to be what they are. In this introduction the findings of the essays in this volume are compared with those of the studies described in Ellen Webster's annotated bibliography, in order to assess what we have found out and what we still need to know about each of the three themes around which this book has been organized.

Christian Images of Women

The images of women held by Christian men and women can and do affect the roles that women play within the churches, as well as the roles that churches play in changing or maintaining the prevailing status of women in general. Much less direct scholarly attention has been paid to this theme than to our other two themes. Moreover, all the essays on this theme that are included here or that are mentioned in the bibliography have been written by historians who have relied on documentary evidence to describe, with one exception, predominantly earlier Protestant missionary, rather than current Asian, African, or Latin-American, Christian images of women. The earlier missionary image of the Chinese woman as "sufferer" described by Shirley Garrett bears a strong resemblance to the missionary image of the Indian woman as "victim" described by John Webster. Although we have no scholarly work on currently operative Christian images of women in China, Africa, or Latin America, Webster argues that in India they bear a close resemblance to more pervasive Indian images of women. A similar situation may well be prevalent elsewhere in the Third World.

Taken together, these essays raise two questions: What were the roots of the earlier missionary images of Third World women, and have those images died with the passing of the missionary era? In "Images of Chinese Women," Shirley Garrett traces the roots of the images she notes not only to the American backgrounds, vocational necessities, and selective experience of the missionaries themselves, but also to the diversities and changing realities of Chinese womanhood over a hundred-year period. In an earlier essay she had argued that feminism was an ideology that missionaries at the turn of the century brought to their work in Japan and China, a conclusion with which the Webster essay is in essential agreement, whereas Deborah Gaitskell has argued that the ideology of domesticity, also imported from overseas, dominated missionary planning in South Africa during roughly the same period.[8] Clearly not all missionaries adopted the same Western images and ideologies or applied them to identical Third World situations. Clearly, also, missionary images and ideologies did not remain static, but changed with changes both in the West and in the Third World societies in which missionaries labored. What is not clear, however, are the details and configurations; more research is needed in this area.

The Webster article shows not only that continuities and changes exist between earlier missionary and present Indian Christian images of women but also that the conscious reference points for developing present images are either current Indian or recent ecumenical Christian, rather than earlier missionary images of Indian women. As the essay points out, images of women are implicit in the roles the churches have been assigning to women and in the kinds of work the churches have been doing for women. Thus this theme cannot be isolated from the other two themes of the book.

The Role of Women in the Church

Recent scholarly literature on the role of women in the Roman Catholic Church, with the exception of Stella Faria's chapter 5, "Catholic Women of India," is devoted almost exclusively to the role of women religious. Several studies of colonial Latin America indicate that nuns—whether Spanish, Indian, or Creole—were cloistered and so played no obvious role in the life of the wider church.[9] A major, and virtually unique, exception to this rule was Sor Juana Inés de la Cruz (1651–1695). In chapter 3, about this first woman theologian in the Americas, Beatriz Couch describes both the opposition Sor Juana had to overcome and the contribution she made in playing a most unusual role in the seventeenth-century church.

A lot of unresearched history remains between Sor Juana and the women religious in Chile whom Katherine Gilfeather describes in chapter 4, "Coming of Age in a Latin Church." By bringing together four earlier studies, each based on extensive interviews with predominantly women religious between 1966 and 1983, and relating her findings to events in the Chilean and Roman Catholic Church at large, Gilfeather shows not only how the role of women religious has been expanded, and their view of the church changed, but also how they have moved since Vatican II from social isolation to solidarity with the poor.

The situation in Chile that Gilfeather examines represents one end of the post–Vatican II spectrum. Africa, where women religious continue to struggle to get out from under the authority of either the European sisters in international orders or the male diocesan hierarchy in the case of the local African orders, represents the other end of the spectrum. There the African sisters have not yet achieved the autonomy they need in order to resolve conflicts between their "African" and their "sister" identities and discover an authentic apostolic identity for themselves.[10] The Indian situation described by Stella Faria seems closer to that of the African than the Chilean sisters because, although aware of the need to move in the Chilean direction, Indian sisters still face serious problems of dependence and cultural alienation. In addition, Faria indicates that Indian laywomen, at both the individual and the organizational levels, are also still caught in a bind between dependency and subordination within hierarchy on the one hand and autonomy with expanded roles on the other.

If the situation of the Roman Catholic women religious provides the most clear-cut example of an externally imposed set of roles within the church for Third World women, the new religions of Africa described by Bennetta Jules-Rosette in chapter 6 provide the best example of female roles within the church that have purely indigenous roots. Jules-Rosette, using both her own and other field research, shows that women have been and still are exercising ceremonial leadership within these new religions. In this respect the "independent," or "separatist," churches grant women a more significant role than do the Roman Catholic and Protestant "mission churches" in Africa.[11] However, Jules-Rosette points out that, in the new religions, women's leadership is restricted to the ceremonial sphere and does not carry over into either the government of these churches or the actual social practice of their members.

The role of Third World women in the churches created by the nineteenth- and twentieth-century Protestant missionary enterprise is less well documented. Both the Webster chapter and a study of Oceania by Charles Forman indicate that women are moving, albeit slowly and with difficulty, into positions of responsibility in the governing bodies and ceremonial leadership of churches of this type.[12] Something of what this has meant for the women involved is seen in chapter 7, Constance Parvey's "Third World Women and Men: Effects of Cultural Change on Interpretation of Scripture," which is based on two World Council of Churches consultations on the Community of Women and Men in the Church, one in Asia and one in Africa. Parvey shows how Third World women are re-visioning the biblical message about men and women by interpreting the scripture "in light of their own self-reliance, empowerment, and experience, not filtered through the eyes of male bias in their own cultures or through the eyes of those who have brought a culturally biased Christianity to them."

What empirical literature we have on the role of Third World women in the churches is focused primarily on the present. From it there emerges a picture of complexity and diversity according to both region[13] and denomination. What is lacking is an adequate historical perspective. A critical area for such research in determining the relative significance of foreign and indigenous influences is, where applicable, the impact of the transfer of power from foreign missionary to indigenous church leadership on the roles of women in the new church structures.

The Church and the Status of Women

The third theme of this book, the role the church has played in affecting the status of Third World women in general, is the theme most directly related to the Third World concerns about women expressed at the Sheffield and EATWOT conferences referred to earlier. It is based on the premise that churches in Third World countries can, if they desire to do so, have an impact on the wider societies of which they are a part and on the relationships between men and women within those societies. Mark Ratkus, in chapter 8, "Women in Philippine Basic Christian Communities," examines one deliberate attempt by the Roman Catholic Church to liberate the oppressed and assesses its impact on women—a fresh approach to the evaluation of Basic (or Base) Christian Communities (BCCs). He shows that the BCCs were politically and economically progressive but socially conservative. They did not see changing the status of women as part of their mission. Moreover, by acting on the unconscious assumption that what was good for the community as a whole would also be good for the women, the BCCs failed to make an impact on the roles and images of women.

Other studies of present-day Colombia, India, and Sierra Leone indicate that there, too, the church has not seen changing the status of women as part of its mission and so it has simply contributed to the maintenance of the status quo.[14] Some studies on southern Africa show how the churches have responded, intentionally or otherwise, to urbanization and industrialization by helping women to cope with the dynamics and consequences of those changes.[15] On the other hand, historical studies, especially of Protestant missions in the nineteenth and early twentieth centuries, have pointed out that the missions not only deliberately sought to improve the status of women but also enjoyed some successes in this regard. The role the missions played in educating and modernizing women leadership in Asian and African countries is well documented, as are their efforts to remove such social evils as footbinding in China and female circumcision in East Africa and to improve the treatment of widows in India and several African countries. However, some of their "successes" have had ambiguous consequences, especially in Africa, where, for example, both Christian marriage law and church-sponsored education for sex-differentiated work roles have led to an economic marginalization that many African women had not experienced previously.[16]

One is left wondering why Christians in Third World countries have apparently moved away from trying to initiate changes in the status of women. Is this caused by a shift in mission priorities consequent upon the transfer of power from foreign missions, where missionary women had a voice in determining policy, to national churches that are dominated by men? Is it because of pervasive unhappiness with missionary blunders in this sphere of social and cultural life or because of a positive desire to indigenize church life? Is it a result of a general pessimism about the churches' ability to introduce meaningful change into this, as into other, areas of national life? Has such pessimism been well founded? Are the constraints exclusively national and local, or are they international as well? Would the answers to these questions be the same for all parts of the Third World? Clearly, this matter bears further systematic investigation.

Although large gaps still exist in our present knowledge of the relationship of the churches and women in Third World countries, perhaps we are now in a position to see some patterns emerge in this relationship. Such insights provide a basis for formulating useful questions and hypotheses for further investigation of this subject. Equally important, what systematic knowledge we have developed about the "whats and whys" of past and present relationships between the churches and women can, like the insights of the theologians and the ethicists, inform decisions concerning what future relationships in particular contexts ought to be, how we can move from the present into that future, and who should play what role in the process.

I
CHRISTIAN IMAGES
OF WOMEN

1

Images
of Chinese Women

Shirley S. Garrett

One of the rare biographies of a Chinese woman published in English is *A Daughter of Han,* written by the medical missionary Ida Pruitt. Between 1936 and 1938, Miss Pruitt had a series of conversations with an energetic old woman named Mrs. Ning, who looked back on her long life as mistreated wife, destitute mother, beggar, peddler, and servant. "I have suffered bitterly," said Mrs. Ning at the beginning of the book. "I have suffered hunger and I have suffered the sight of my children sold. All have I had in a superlative degree."[1] Her story went on to prove it. Enduring, hardworking, meeting one terrible crisis after another, she was unquestionably the noble Chinese woman sufferer so well known to the American Protestant church consciousness, and she was only one of many. Of the Chinese woman, Helen Barrett Montgomery wrote for the church in 1910, "She is not desired at birth, is subject to father, husband and son."[2] In 1920, in a church tract called *Chinese Heartthrobs,* a story entitled "Paying for Oneself" told of a woman who was sold by not just one but by two husbands in turn and forced to work in the fields to pay off her own purchase price.[3] In 1928 an industrial study conducted under church auspices recorded how women slaved in silk and match factories up to twenty hours a day. One of the workers was described as "a drooping little girl of seven or eight years of age . . . with swollen body and mask-like face of helpless suffering."[4] With such accounts, it was no wonder that the image of suffering Chinese women was sharply imprinted on the Western mind.

Not far into *A Daughter of Han,* however, the reader comes across another side of Mrs. Ning: her hot temper. When she was thirteen, her mother whipped her for being disobedient. As a broom came down on her head the child shouted, "I dare to do it again, I dare to do it again."[5] From an episode later in life, Mrs. Ning remembered the following exchange after a scolding by her mistress:

"I said, 'Let's settle our accounts.'
. . . She said, 'If you have a good place to go, go.'
'If I haven't a place to go, I'll beg.' So I left."⁶

By the time *A Daughter of Han* appeared in print, both the submissive
role and the assertive personality of the Chinese women were known to
missionaries, who provided raw material for the church's image of Chinese womanhood. Missionaries had had extensive experience as educators, healers, and employers and could comprehend both the general
roles and the individual personalities around them. It was, however, the
Chinese woman as sufferer of whom they first tended to speak, and it was
the sufferer who dominated the American consciousness well into the
twentieth century. When they described her personality, it was in terms
of her fortitude and those sides of her nature that they found admirable.
Her more militant side was not usually talked about, any more than were
the manipulators, the sexual libertines, or the criminals who people Mrs.
Ning's colorful world of memories. As a result, the Protestant church's
Chinese woman often seemed one-dimensional, a disembodied role
rather than a real person.

When the last imperial dynasty was overthrown, in 1911, and a republic of sorts emerged, a new type of woman began to appear with growing
frequency, especially among the middle classes. She was a being more
complex to understand and explain. When she fit into the church's
accepted models of womanhood or remained visible as a sufferer, the
church was comfortable. Confronted by the militant, the sensualist, the
revolutionary, the church was ill at ease or silent. Self-imposed illusions,
some common to all image making and some rooted in the special needs
and preconceptions of the church in America, made it difficult to accept
the wide varieties of women who began to appear after the 1911 revolution. What missionaries emphasized in their reports became increasingly
different from what they saw, and those reports were sometimes translated into an even more skewed picture for missionary supporters at
home. Along with the wishful thinking, however, there were real insights
about women in a modernizing society. Thus, although the church encounter with Chinese women on what is today termed mainland China
lies well in the past, the experience provided many lessons that are
relevant for the church in its work with women today.

I

The image of the Chinese woman as sufferer was potent and enduring
for many reasons. First of all, American audiences were easily persuaded
of its truth. As early as the 1830s but in greater degree after the American

Civil War, missionaries to China sent back indignant stories about the sorry lives of girls and grown women. They reported a society in which girl babies were sometimes killed and frequently abandoned, a practice so persistent that as late as 1909 the Reverend William Edwin Hoy wrote that someone offered him and his wife two babies. The Hoys reluctantly turned the infants down, since they were already supporting another abandoned girl, but he feared the fate of the babies and wrote, "The cries of the two little ones pierce my soul, I can never get away from them."[7] Little girls brought to missionary schools were often taken away at age eight or ten and sent to work or sometimes to brothels, a practice still reported in 1917. Girls had their feet bound, a custom both Westerners and Manchu rulers found unhealthy and repellent. Marriages were arranged by relatives and often contracted for when girls were still babies. At about eighteen, even girls from poor families were secluded in their households, shut off in women's quarters from a larger society. Wives were often mistreated by their husbands and sometimes sold by them, and concubines were taken into households in which there was already a wife. Missionaries were particularly struck by the high incidence of suicide among young married women, who were under the absolute control of husbands and mothers-in-law. Only by bearing a son and becoming a mother-in-law herself did a woman achieve status and power. It was not hard to see suffering as the central theme of a Chinese woman's life, and this rich vein was mined exhaustively by mission reporters. Indeed, such stories, verified by Western and Chinese historians and journalists, were subsequently emphasized by the Communist regime in its denunciations of traditional Chinese society.

The image of suffering women was particularly striking because, for a time, it was the only image of Chinese women that was presented by the church. Most of these early sad stories reflected the lives of the destitute, and it was the destitute whom missionaries first encountered. There were plenty of them. War, floods, famine, opium introduced by the West, and political disruption were causing continuing turmoil in China after the mid-nineteenth century. At such times all poor people were vulnerable, and women and girls were considered the most expendable. In the vast assortment of economic and social classes found in China, women were strictly controlled but not uniformly maltreated. Although foot-binding, seclusion, and arranged marriages were widespread, the well-to-do and the working poor did not kill their female babies or sell their daughters. Mrs. Ning, hovering on the edge of impoverishment, fought desperately to keep one daughter from being sold by her drug-addicted husband. In most of China, women did not do hard labor in the fields. If young women were secluded, it was felt to be for their own protection.

But neither did people with any defenses originally have anything to do with missionaries, who were initially feared or despised. Mrs. Ning remembered that people in her town would not at first rent or sell houses to missionaries, and throughout China it was for a while difficult to get girls even from poor families to enroll in mission schools, although teachers offered free tuition and keep. Evangelization was strongly resisted; as Mrs. Ning remarked and many reports confirmed, only when the crops failed and there was no food was it convenient to believe. As the missionary reputation for philanthropy, medical assistance, and teaching spread, hostility receded among the poor, but not until the eve of the twentieth century did most missionaries have much contact with the more prosperous Chinese. It was thus the vision of the poor, of suffering at its most intense, that provided the first impression. This impression long stood for China as a whole in some quarters of the church, and it is fair to say that it was always the predominant image of Chinese women for the larger American church audience.

As missionaries began to meet Chinese women who were more prosperous, they could identify them, too, as sufferers, if of a different kind from the poor. By the end of the nineteenth century, exhortations to educate women for their own good and the good of China came not only from missionaries but also from progressive Chinese, and the education of middle-class girls began to spread. Many of these girls went to missionary schools, since at first there were few others. As encounters began to multiply, missionaries became acquainted with a different class of women from the ones they had previously known. These middle-class girls and their older relatives wore fine clothes, ate fine foods, were waited on by many servants, and were fussed over and protected. Nevertheless, many seemed to lead lives that were empty and constricted, with no future but the prospects of servility to a husband and mother-in-law and the hope of bearing sons. All they could do, wrote one missionary, was read novels if they could read, attend private theatricals, and gamble.[8] To missionary women, they too seemed oppressed, a conviction echoed by Chinese women writers in the 1920s, who described their own desperate urge as girls to become educated and to escape from arranged marriages and the power of relatives.[9] Thus middle-class Chinese women could also be fitted into the overall image of suffering.

The image of the sufferer was crucial to the success of the China mission, for it had great appeal and usefulness to the churchwomen in America who supported that mission so faithfully. Work for poor Chinese women and girls offered a worthy outlet for the humanitarianism that was one central theme of Christianity, reflecting the Christian ideal of service. Work for Chinese women was also a way of expressing and extending the moderate feminism of women in the churches to their oppressed sisters overseas. In addition, helping and liberating foreign women was a bond of solidarity for women in mission societies because it gave them a focus and a reason for existence as a female stronghold. After their work during the American Civil War, churchwomen seeking larger roles at home had been nudged into domestic and foreign missionary work rather than into church administration. Women's mission societies became the major expression of female importance within the church. It was women, they told themselves, who could best work to liberate other women. Thus it was natural that the plight of women abroad should be a primary concern, responsible for the flowering in China, India, and the Middle East of girls' schools, women's hospitals, refuges, and campaigns for health and protection. By any yardstick such accomplishments are praiseworthy. It does not diminish the work or the sentiments motivating it to say that American mission societies also needed to see these Chinese, Indian, or Islamic women as sufferers to justify their own feminist urges.[10]

The problem with the image of sufferer, however, was that it carried with it theological and cultural nuances that made special behavioral demands. In Christianity the suffering woman was supposed to learn from adversity and be the better for it—what one Chinese Christian woman termed "a creative concept of suffering and redemption."[11] In 1910 Helen Montgomery described a Chinese Bible woman approvingly as "a gentle little woman . . . whose refined face shows lines of trial and the sweet chastening which comes from a hard fight in a hard place, for Christ's sake."[12] Years later Pearl Buck, born of missionary parents, wrote that it was oppression that had produced the best qualities of the Chinese woman, her fortitude and capacity for hard work.[13] This picture of the gentle but sturdy Chinese sufferer was appealing to middle-class American women, who valued the same qualities. A "good" Chinese sufferer could engage their sympathy, admiration, and support. If she also exhibited "womanliness," by which missionaries meant docility, modesty, and chasteness, her image would be even more engaging.

Fortunately, there were plenty of "good" sufferers around. The docile and womanly yet capable woman was an ideal type in China too, celebrated in a number of famous books of maxims on the proper behavior for women. This ideal type was by no means a figment of the imagination. Such women existed in large numbers. Consequently, it was easy for missionaries to perceive and discuss the Chinese woman's fortitude, character, and gentleness. The prosperous Chinese woman in particular emerged on the American consciousness as a compendium of admirable qualities—gentleness, modesty, graciousness, piquancy, charm, reserve —an image enhanced by the porcelain-skinned, delicate Chinese girls who came to study in the United States and sometimes spoke beguilingly before mission societies. Their personality traits seemed an excellent foundation for the woman of the future. The church dreamed that fundamental Chinese excellence, plus its own work of education, philanthropy, and character building, would help to produce a new Chinese woman, free from her many oppressions yet noble in character and aspiration. This woman could emerge if traditional Chinese attitudes were properly transformed and Christian ideals put in their place.

Missionaries blamed the low status of Chinese women on the traditional Confucian order that for centuries had shaped Chinese attitudes. From the long and endlessly interpreted dogma of Confucianism, they were fond of picking out the phrase "the place of woman is to respect, obey, submit to authority." In the non-Christian world great social injustices were sanctioned by the recognized standards of the people, wrote Helen Montgomery. With women regarded so contemptuously, it would always be difficult to raise their status. A change in the heart of society, a kind of spiritual revolution, would have to take place. This inner change could be brought about by Christianity, for the Bible honored women. Spreading Christian ideals in Chinese society would spread a sense of the dignity and value of women and encourage freedom and new opportunities for them.[14] It would also influence women themselves. In the individual life it would bring a sense of personal worth. The doleful heroine of "Paying for Oneself," when asked how she had survived her travail, answered that she kept saying, "Jesus loved me, someone loved me."[15] Moreover, Christian influence would encourage women to serve others, not only in the familiar role of mother, but also as teachers, doctors, nurses, and social workers. The new woman would not only receive but give as well. It was hoped that such ideals would spread among all Chinese women, but the transforming power of Christianity would be most evident in the convert, who would embody the highest standards of womanhood. The Christian mother, teacher, or healer would be a radiant testimony to the power of the gospel.

From these missionary dreams emerged the public image of the Chinese Christian woman. Some of the real stories of Chinese Christians are admirable—it took courage and dedication to become the first woman doctor in China or to be a Bible woman in an indifferent or hostile society. Yet even when viewed sympathetically, missionary descriptions of Chinese Christians strain credibility. The Reverend F. L. Hawks Pott wrote of Chinese men, "The Christians are differentiated from the non-Christians. Many of them lead lives which are the admiration and wonder of those who do not understand the transforming power of the gospel of Christ."[16] The Christian woman described by churchwoman Margaret Burton was flawless: "attractive, intelligent, refined, spiritual, kind, truthful, helpful, energetic, ambitious in good ways."[17] To Tseng Pao-swen, herself a Christian, she was a special creature, "spiritually purifying and free, . . . pragmatic and positive, and emotionally loving and helpful."[18] Perhaps the most frequently encountered adjective was "radiant." It was an appealing picture indeed, all sunlight and no shadow. If the Chinese woman in general was excellent, the Chinese Christian woman was a saint.

To some extent such exaggeration was inherent in the art of selling any image, but it was not merely public relations at their most calculated. If the American Protestant church was soaked in a sense of sin, it was also bathed in the glow of perennial optimism, the sense of potential perfectibility in every situation. Optimism was basic to missionary work. Thus, both the requirements of the church's public and the dictates of the heart led to reports that were full of hope, and the tracts and pamphlets written in America, often by people who had never been to China, bristled with Chinese women who were quaint, virtuous, and noble, gentle and deserving creatures called Precious Jade and Flowering Lotus. The Chinese Christian woman in particular was featured, with many stories of her growing influence in society and her radiant character. As a result, the Chinese woman, Christian or not, was stripped of her humanity. A cynic would have to look carefully between the lines to see her in three dimensions.

In the flesh, however, she was quite human, and some of her real characteristics were at odds with the cheerful picture the church presented to the public. She was superstitious, believing stubbornly in magic, native gods, and the spells and portents of wind and water and often sullenly resisting attempts to convert her. She was capable of hate and vengefulness, often using threats of suicide to get her own way against a family that feared loss of face if she carried out her threats. She sometimes henpecked her husband or had sexual relations outside of marriage. She had a distressingly hot temper. In 1890 a Chinese convert named Mrs. Ahok warned teachers that Chinese girls would be very difficult to manage in school,[19] and a woman missionary described their mothers as "self-willed, passionate girls."[20] Mrs. Ning fought with her missionary employers. The Reverend S. S. Snyder of the Evangelical and Reformed Church had an angry confrontation with a language teacher because she refused to walk through the streets of Chengchow to school.[21]

To some extent, missionaries were certainly aware of these personality characteristics. In private they recognized the manipulative abilities of some Chinese women. They found that some of their employees were prostitutes on the side (and quickly fired them).[22] They delicately referred to "freedom" in marriage as a code word for sexual compatibility, and they frequently encountered high temper. Yet in public they kept on describing young girls as being "eager" and older ones as being gentle and charming, reserved and modest.

In thus envisaging the new Chinese woman, the church was not prepared for the full range of her possibilities, for all that she might be capable of becoming out of her own nature. It did not grasp that Chinese, rather than Western, personality traits and values would determine what she wanted to be, how she would decide to serve. When she emerged, neither her chosen role nor her personality was always what the church expected or hoped for.

II

Although the new Chinese woman seemed to burst upon the scene in 1919, variations of the traditional stereotypes had already been appearing. There were always a few accomplished and educated women. There were even a few rebels like the famous Ch'iu Chin, who left her husband and children in 1904 and went to study in Japan, where she dressed in men's clothing and flourished a sword. Less daring girls went with increasing frequency to missionary schools and after 1905 flocked to the schools at last being established by the Chinese themselves. They became literate, took part at first reluctantly and then enthusiastically in athletics, cut their hair, and began to learn about life in the outside world. Girls began to appear on the streets, foot-binding became unfashionable in urban areas, and young men began to look for modern, educated wives. There was even a small women's movement in 1906. China's most celebrated modern woman writer, Ding Ling, wrote that by 1913 her own mother, having won the battles against foot-binding and lack of education, had paved the way for a new generation of girls who took these victories for granted and turned to fighting for freedom in marriage and a wide range of women's rights.[23]

Missionaries who had helped to create progressive attitudes applauded these changes, praising the combination of dignity, modesty, and real accomplishment that they discerned in the new woman. In 1919 the American missionary Mary Gamewell wrote of the modern Chinese woman that she was poised, effective in public, yet still had "modest womanliness."[24]

Yet other results of liberation were appearing. Now that girls and boys were meeting socially, the much vaunted modesty of Chinese girls seemed to be disappearing. Hawks Pott wrote: "Boldness and boisterousness often take the place of the gentleness and modesty for which she has always been renowned. Unaccustomed to the free intermingling of the sexes there is grave danger lest her liberty may not too often lead to her ruin." He cited a Miss Lambert's report of an entertainment that had in fact led to the "moral ruin" of most of the girls.[25]

Equally dismaying to the missionaries was the rise of what seemed to be a new type of woman, the militant. Within the range of stock heroines that were available to Chinese women, one was in fact the woman warrior. Her modern counterpart now began to emerge. There were a few women revolutionaries in China at the turn of the century. Ch'iu Chin returned to China to become a revolutionary, was executed in 1907, and became a national heroine. In 1903 women took part in anti-Russian demonstrations; in 1911 a group of women were actually part of the revolutionary army that overthrew imperial rule. Immediately afterward, a group of militant feminists emerged. In 1912, after a women's suffrage organization petitioned the newly established Parliament for equal rights, a number of young women stormed the Parliament building, broke windows, and injured some guards. There were strikes by girls at Chinese and missionary schools over such issues as curricula and holidays. Missionaries did not take kindly to this aspect of the new woman. Hawks Pott wrote that "Chinese suffragettes . . . resorted to the same violent methods of window smashing as their sisters in the British Isles."[26] Margaret Burton wrote that sudden access to freedom had led girl students to "regrettably high-handed methods of expressing themselves."[27]

Still, these seemed isolated types, for most of the women with whom missionaries were dealing fell into more familiar categories. In the smaller towns, little seemed to have changed. In the inland city of Yochow, a missionary wrote in 1917 that one of her students, a girl of twelve, had been brought to her black and blue, beaten by a mother-in-law who was anxious to get rid of her. Another student had been saved from being sold to "a notoriously bad man."[28] Chinese teachers in the city still lived at school because they could not go out onto the streets, and the desperately poor women in a nearby village still turned to prostitution as the only way to earn money.

The sufferer was also increasingly evident in the big cities, where the innovative YWCA prodded the church to turn its attention to the thousands of women and children who were toiling in sweatshops under conditions so inhuman that in 1924 more than a hundred women were burned to death in a silk filature where the doors were locked. If suffering was taking place in a new context, the image of suffering itself was familiar. Familiar and laudable, too, were the stories of YWCA workers, Western and Chinese, who went into the mills to run clinics on health and child care.

Well-to-do women at first seemed a new breed. Initially, many of them appeared to be merely caught up in the trappings of modernity at its most superficial. Students returning from the West congregated in Canton, where the writer Nora Waln remembered that they "danced to victrola records, played tennis, raced speedboats, flirted, and theorized continuously about what they would do with their learning as soon as they got the opportunity." She also remembered one friend coming to show off her new windblown bob and an orange voile dress from Paris that came only to her knees.[29] But these young society women seemed intelligent and committed as they talked knowledgeably about politics and reform, and some of them, including Mei-ling Soong, the future Madame Chiang Kai-shek, worked in Shanghai on a number of social service projects.

But along with these types, the dead-serious radical feminist was now making an appearance, and she was less appealing to missionary sensibilities. With the onset of the famous May Fourth Movement in China in 1919, an intoxication with new ideas began to emerge among students and intellectuals, female as well as male. One aspect of this was a brief flourishing of feminist writing in which young writers described with unprecedented candor[30] the sexual longings, loveless marriages, and unwanted pregnancies of the middle-class Chinese woman. Soon the mood turned from introspection to action. As the new Communist movement began to provide a blueprint for the future that promised swift and effective remedies for women as well as for China, feminists began to base their hopes for true equality on political revolution rather than on discussion groups, slow-moving government reforms, or Christian ideals. There were violent strikes at both government and missionary schools, demonstrations for feminism in the streets, and the formation of militant women's associations in several provinces. The virulently antireligious communism of the period and the hot impatience of the young produced a wave of anti-Christian demonstrations that shook the missionary community.

The church could glimpse the reasoning behind strikes and demonstrations by women in the industrial sweatshops, who launched an abortive attempt to get better working conditions for themselves and their children. For militant feminism, especially when associated with radical politics, the church had little stomach. How should the new woman be understood? In June of 1925, when Shanghai feminists threatened to hold a protest demonstration if the Peking government ignored demands for equal treatment, the *Chinese Recorder,* which spoke for the missionary movement, tried to be reassuring. There was indeed, the *Recorder* editorialist wrote, a women's rights association seeking legal protection for Chinese women and urging their active participation in public affairs. Most such groups, however, came and went; of those that persisted, such as the Women's Christian Temperance Union (WCTU) and the YWCA, most were Christian. In undergraduate life, Chinese girls showed both types of "student initiative," the kind that joined men students in striking and the "normal kind that works with the YWCA." The *Recorder* believed that the women's movement in China was both bad and good: "At some points it goes too fast to be substantial or bring permanent good but on the whole it would seem to be here to stay. At any rate it is one of the greatest forces in China to be reckoned with and welcomed by the Christian church."[31] The impression left by the editorial was that the militant woman was in fact an aberration, and that the "normal kind" who worked in moderate reform programs was the real new woman.

The troubling question of militant women was to be dealt with shortly and summarily by the Chinese themselves as tumultuous political events swept the radical feminist into official oblivion. In 1927 Chiang Kai-shek mobilized conservative support for a military campaign that would include wiping out Communist sympathizers and restoring order to a turbulent society. In the violence that overtook the country, missionaries were forced to withdraw. As Chiang assumed a shaky control, they returned to find that the new government was curbing all evidences of unruliness. The next few years were to see brutal reprisals against militant feminists and an attempt to restore the womanly woman and the social servant to center stage.

The Nationalist government under Chiang did not intend to tolerate any organizations it could not dominate. Therefore, Chiang mobilized all women's associations into strictly controlled government organizations. Moreover, the new regime had an austere traditional streak that led it to look with disfavor on some aspects of the modern woman. An English churchwoman noted official views when she collected a pamphlet at a government-organized mass meeting in honor of International Woman's Day in 1928. "The meaning of the women's movement," said the pamphlet, "is not to annihilate masculine strength—not to put an end to the grace of women's nature or evade the function of motherhood."[32] A spokeswoman for the regime wrote for an American church audience, "The modern Chinese woman has often mistaken her true position. She tries to be a replica of man."[33] In an attempt to reinstate the old values that were still dear to many Chinese, dancing was forbidden in some cities, women with bobbed hair and Western clothes were attacked, and men and women were forbidden to walk arm in arm in public.

Furthermore, the government clamped down on militant feminists who had any connection with radical politics, whether through writing about social problems or through direct political activity. Feminist writers were persecuted, and female revolutionaries were arrested and executed, along with their male counterparts. Some women fled to the cave village of Yenan, where Mao-Tse-tung was reputedly establishing a

Communist society in which women would be equal to men. Most simply kept quiet. Political involvement was dangerous, and in the area of China in which the church functioned, the assertive, politicized woman faded from view.

In the subdued climate, church organizations dealing with women still found much to be cheerful about. The new Madame Chiang Kai-shek was the American-educated Mei-ling Soong, daughter of a prominent and powerful Christian family and the symbol of modern Chinese Christian womanhood to the church. Madame Chiang moved to include the church in a government program of social service that was eagerly embraced by missionaries. The YWCA was held in high repute, sending its workers into rural villages to work with women and children and continuing its moderate remedial programs in the urban areas. The government passed a new legal code that, on paper, gave women equality with men, allowing them to share the family inheritance, guaranteeing free choice in marriage between individuals, and outlawing concubinage and sale of women. Women moved into many professions, ranging from banking to police work. Young girls freely discussed love and sex, and the YWCA sponsored a lecture on birth control in Shanghai in 1933. Chinese women, wrote Mrs. Herman Liu for the *Chinese Recorder* in 1934, were new beings, free human creatures like men. To judge by such cheerful reports, the new Chinese woman under the Nationalist regime fulfilled many of the dreams that Helen Montgomery had voiced years before, and the Chinese Christian woman in particular was in the forefront, leading and serving society.

But in fact the tone was darkening, even among women who were dedicated to Christian service. A woman rural worker for the church went over to the Communists. Cora Deng, a YWCA secretary, wrote bitterly about conditions in the mills, lashing out at profiteering by millowners. Mrs. Ning's granddaughter, educated by missionaries in China and America and now a teacher, telling her grandmother that a new day was coming when the people of China would rule themselves, disappeared into the hills, where Communist guerrillas were beginning to fight against Japanese invaders. As the twin specters of domestic unrest and Japanese war darkened the air, even the "normal kind" of woman was changing in unexpected ways.

All this was of less and less concern to a church community in America that was somewhat disillusioned with China and was struggling with the effects of the Depression. Who the Chinese woman was and what she wanted was no longer very important, even within the church. The sympathetic support of the American church was, however, important to China in its struggle to mobilize public opinion in the United States against Japan. In the mid-1930s Madame Chiang launched a formidable campaign to gain that support by reviving the old emotional appeals. A vigorous public relations effort in America portrayed Madame Chiang as Christian mother to an entire nation, as a spiritual influence on her husband, and as a rescuer of suffering Chinese children. A barrage of books and articles tried to reanimate through this image of suffering and service the traditional American sense of responsibility for China, particularly for its girls and women. Some within the church were still responsive, and a faithful group followed missionary work in China during the war with interest. The story of the colleges that moved from the occupied cities to Free China were especially appealing, and young Chinese girls again stood for heroism and fortitude in the midst of travail.

But it was late in the day. With the end of the Japanese war, China was launched upon a civil war that ended in the Communist takeover. It soon became evident that there would be no place for foreign missionaries in the new society, and they had to leave. From 1950 on there would be no more firsthand church encounters with Chinese women, or anything else Chinese, for many years. If the church thought about contemporary Chinese women at all, it would have to borrow its images from elsewhere.

III

It takes no great insight to say that the church's images of women had been a composite of the real and the fanciful, selective in China and somewhat fantasized in America. From the Chinese experience the church can extract its own lessons about evaluating women of other cultures too superficially. It is more fruitful here to look at the larger implications of the church's encounter with Chinese women, dated though the experience may seem at first to be.

For one thing, the church experience with Chinese women drives home the realization that it is impossible to know the implications of any new influence. Change begets the unexpected, and women in different societies will react from their own singular needs and expectations. This happened in China, and it will happen everywhere that church workers or social engineers go with their dreams and plans. The new woman will turn out to be a surprise, and not always a welcome one.

For another, the Chinese experience is a reminder that change begets resistance. Deep traditional attitudes are hard to shake no matter what the political system may be. The new woman whom missionaries saw developing was in many ways anathema to conservative Chinese values, which transcended politics. The Nationalist government clipped her wings. The Communist government, too, has rigid standards of behavior. Personal modesty, chastity, and social discipline are as valued in China today as they were by Confucianists and missionaries a hundred years ago. Marriage still requires approval, by society if not by family. Despite many improvements in their legal rights, women in China still feel the impact of old attitudes, ranging from the common burdens of work, shopping, and household duties to the rumored recurrence of female infanticide in a society that is trying to limit families to one child apiece. Modernization of a traditional society is apt to generate a reverse impulse, as we have recently seen in Iran.

Moreover, modernization exacts its own price. The old-fashioned woman in China, betrothed at an early age and poorly educated, became a helpless victim of the new society, often divorced by her modern husband and unequipped for the changing times. The highly educated new woman was suspect and could not find a husband at all, even though she usually wanted to marry. The radical feminists who went to join the Communists in Yenan found that, although they were rid of the burdensome tyranny of their families, they now had the equally awesome burden of personal autonomy, in which they had to be responsible for their own choices and live with them. Such problems are the inevitable by-products of any changing society, and the church will encounter them again in the future.

Finally, if by no means exhaustively, the varied search by Chinese women for "true equality" is a demonstration of how elusive and indefinable this term is. The feminist writers of the 1920s admitted to the realization that perhaps there were inescapable contradictions in a woman's life, conflicting goals that no system could solve, revolutionary or not. With often incompatible demands of personal emotion versus work, dependence versus freedom, it was hard to pin down what true equality was, or even if it could be achieved in an imperfect world. Equality seemed to have a different definition, and a different value, for different women. As the church works today in modernizing societies, women will continue to find the definition of equality difficult. As a result, their aspirations and choices may startle the church, and all of us.

2

Assumptions About the Indian Woman Underlying Protestant Church Policies and Programs, 1947–1982

John C. B. Webster

What is the Indian woman really like? What does God intend her to become? What therefore is her proper place and role in the life and mission of the church? The primary purpose of this chapter is not to provide answers to those questions but, by analyzing the assumptions about the Indian woman underlying church policies and programs, to indicate how in fact the Protestant churches have answered them since India became an independent country. A secondary purpose is to discover whether there is anything distinctively Indian or Christian in these assumptions. The first section of the chapter provides the historical context for this inquiry. The next two sections are devoted to an examination of the publications and records first of the National Christian Council of India, an ecumenical organization of non–Roman Catholic churches, so as to get as broad a range of Protestant opinion and practice as possible, and then of the Church of South India, probably the largest single Protestant church in India, for a more detailed case study. The concluding section will relate the findings of the preceding sections to each other and then assess their significance by comparing them to those of other studies of Indian women.

I

Scholars generally trace the origins of the women's movement in India to the nineteenth-century reformers who sought to improve the condition of women by establishing schools for girls as well as by publicly opposing female infanticide, the early age of marriage and of consent, and the prohibition against widow remarriage. Whether this activity was primarily the result of the general permeation of Western ideas among the educated elite, a response to the threat social change posed to traditional Indian family life, or a reaction to missionary criticisms is a matter of scholarly debate.[1]

Certainly nineteenth-century Protestant missionaries raised "the women's issue" in their apologetic for Christianity by making the better treatment Christians accorded to women an important "evidence" of the truth of Christianity and the falsity of other religions. Moreover, as if to substantiate their claims, they became increasingly committed to four types of "women's work" as the century progressed: evangelism; education, where their contribution especially at levels above the primary stage was enormous; medical work, which by 1900 surpassed missionary medical work among men; and rescue work among widows, fallen women, and famine victims. They also joined with like-minded Hindus in demanding social reform legislation to improve the Indian woman's lot.

Underlying these efforts was the assumption that the Indian woman was a victim of religiously sanctioned social custom, ignorance, and neglect. However, the life that God intended for her, while often summed up in the biblical metaphor of leaven, was in fact that of the middle- to upper-middle-class Victorian woman from whose ranks the missionary women were themselves drawn. The Indian woman could, if converted, emulate this model. She could live a purer, more uplifting life; she could become educated; she could thus become either a companion instead of a mere servant to her husband or a useful mission worker; she could become a better mother; she could be a noble example to and a beneficent influence upon society at large.

The women's movement entered its second stage after World War I when Indian women not only joined the nationalist struggle in large numbers at Mahatma Gandhi's invitation but also formed organizations of their own, which were recognized as the chief voices of Indian womanhood.[2] During this stage, Protestant "women's work" remained basically the same but the assumptions underlying it were modified. Both foreign and Indian Protestants adopted a more positive attitude toward Indian religions and recognized that the Indian woman's situation was changing. While Protestants felt that they had been catalysts of these changes, they also believed that the ordinary Indian woman's lot continued to be a very hard one. God still intended the Indian woman to be leaven, with the important proviso that she remain an Indian, combining in her person the highest Indian ideals of womanhood with the invigorating and discerning powers the gospel bestows.[3]

Thus Protestant assumptions about the Indian woman continued to be directed outward: the non-Christian woman was a victim and the Christian woman was leaven in Indian society as a whole. It did not seem to cross anyone's mind that the Indian woman might be both victim and leaven within the church itself! Missionary women had an assured place as decision makers within their missions, and what influence Indian women enjoyed and the contributions they made were due to their responsibilities within mission structures. However, following Independence, when power was transferred from foreign missions, in which women had considerable power, to Indian churches, in which they had virtually none, the woman's position within the Protestant churches began to change.

The women's movement appeared to collapse after Independence once the constitution prohibited discrimination on the basis of sex and the Hindu Code Bill of 1956 liberalized the divorce laws and granted inheritance rights to women. It was revitalized and given new direction in 1975 when, as part of the International Women's Year, the Committee on the Status of Women in India issued a report, *Towards Equality*, which concluded that the progress of women since Independence was more apparent than real, as their status had actually declined demographically, politically, and economically, especially in rural areas and unorganized sectors of the economy.

Improvement within the prevailing framework of Indian society is now considered impossible because the traditional patriarchal assumptions of the post-Independence planners, who viewed women in terms of welfare rather than development, proved detrimental to women. Moreover, in this third stage the elitist character of the movement is also being modified as women make greater efforts to mobilize across class lines and establish a broader base for the redress of common grievances. The present movement has no common organization or ideology but, rather, consists of diverse groups seeking, often in different ways, to reverse some of the trends revealed in *Towards Equality*.[4]

II

The National Christian Council of India (NCCI) took little official cognizance of women per se. It had neither a permanent secretary nor a committee on women's work and rarely singled women out for special attention in its general programs. Those NCCI activities that touched women most directly were the Christian Home Movement, established to tie the church and the home closer together, and its efforts to bring the marriage and divorce laws affecting Christians into line with those in the Hindu Code Bill. The result was the Christian Marriage and Matrimonial Causes Bill of 1962, which ultimately failed to pass owing, according to one writer, to opposition in both Roman Catholic and Orthodox Church circles.[5] However, neither the council nor any other church body took steps to make similar changes in the inheritance laws applicable to Christians, even though these were also unfair to women.[6]

According to Kaj Baago, the main concern of the council during the first fifteen years after Independence was the upbuilding of the church.[7] This concern is reflected in the aims of the Christian Home Movement, in two NCCI studies on women published during this period (*The Life and Work of Women in the Church in India and Pakistan* and *The Ministry of Women,* published in 1951 and 1962, respectively),[8] and in the articles on women published in the *National Christian Council Review* from the late 1940s through the 1960s. Thus the council's attention was focused upon the Christian rather than upon the non-Christian woman.

All these sources indicate that traditional patriarchal assumptions about the Indian woman provided the framework within which discussions on the upbuilding of the church took place. The assumption that the Indian Christian woman is a married woman whose primary loyalty is to her family was built into the questionnaire on which the 1951 *Life and Work* survey was based and was also reflected in many of the answers it listed as well as in subsequent articles on the subject.[9] Another assumption was that while the Indian Christian woman was important and influential within her own sphere, that sphere was separate from and subordinate to the world of men. The home was primarily the woman's sphere. In church she sat separately from the men, usually looked after the children during Sunday worship, and rarely held office even when permitted to do so.[10] Women were considered particularly good at certain types of church work—teaching the young and illiterate, secretarial tasks, social work of various kinds—but unhelpful in financial, property, basic policy, and legal-political matters.[11] Women workers labored either among other women, among children, or in backward areas where men rarely went.[12]

What God intended for the Christian woman was partnership with men in the ministry and mission of the church. However, those in charge of training programs for women volunteers or full-time workers found the obstacles to partnership so many and so formidable that they kept wondering out loud what specifically they were really training women for.[13]

The 1970s witnessed considerable questioning of this patriarchal framework when feminist and liberationist theologies and then the International Women's Year made their impact felt on the Protestant churches in India. Conferences were held, the All-India Council of Christian Women was formed and functioned as the "woman's wing" of the NCCI, and the number of articles on Indian women in the *Review* increased. Their authors were now Indian instead of foreign missionary women, and liberation of the oppressed replaced the upbuilding of the church as their dominant theme. They saw women less as hitherto untapped resources for serving the church's institutional objectives than as important in their own right. They directed attention outward once again toward the Indian woman—her status, her dignity, her humanity —but instead of accentuating differences between Christian and non-Christian women in nineteenth-century fashion, these authors stressed their similarities, generally by using the situation of the Christian woman as an example of the more pervasive problems that all Indian women face also, albeit in somewhat different forms.

The assumption that the Indian woman is a victim again predominated: that she is oppressed by men, dependent upon men, the servant of men. Evidence for this was drawn from the home, from religious organizations, and from the workplace. Articles emphasized not the progress women had made but either the widening gap between men and women or the progress yet to be made.[14] They also gave attention to current social evils particularly harmful to women, the dowry system and inheritance laws being the most frequently mentioned.[15] Another common assumption about the Indian woman was that she is poor. This emphasis was strategic, aimed at getting educated Christian women to come out and identify themselves with the poor.[16]

What God intends for the Indian woman is liberation from her bondage, equality with men, full humanity.[17] The biblical texts most frequently cited to support this contention were Genesis 1:27, Galatians 3:28, and, above all, those in the Gospels that showed how Jesus (in sharp contrast to contemporary Jewish society or subsequent Christian practice) treated women. Yet, while acquainted with developments in the West, these authors showed little desire to become like Western women; instead they sought a Christian image of Indian female humanity suitable to Indian realities.

These assumptions had two implications for the ministry and mission of the church: reform and redirection. Because the church was a male-dominated institution whose operative images of women, especially at the popular level, were self-serving male images, women had to be represented more equally in decision-making bodies, and prevailing Christian images of women had to be challenged and replaced.[18] Women's ordination was an important issue for both of those reasons. Moreover, the church's mission should be directed toward poor women; it should identify itself with them in their struggles for a more fully human life.[19]

III

Whereas the NCCI could provide information and forums for discussion about women's issues, decisions affecting women were made by its member churches, the largest of which has been the Church of South

India. In this case study, therefore, assumptions about the Indian woman are inferred not just from consciously stated opinions but also from decisions made or not made.

The Church of South India (CSI), a union of churches from the Anglican, Methodist, Congregational, and Presbyterian traditions, came into being in September 1947. Because neither the role of women in the new church nor the impact that that union might have upon women or women's work was discussed during the negotiating period,[20] arrangements for women were made after the new church was already in existence. These arrangements were the Women's Fellowship of the Church of South India and the Order for Women in the Church of South India, established in 1948 and 1952, respectively.

Three of the four original objectives of the Women's Fellowship dealt with the Christian home and family, the fourth being "to unite members in prayer, service and witness."[21] Despite the predominantly domestic orientation of these objectives, reports of the fellowship's activities stressed its role in the Christian nurture of members, in evangelism, in service-oriented efforts to bridge gaps between urban educated women and rural women, and especially in building greater unity at the grass roots among members of the uniting churches. During the 1950s it even entertained hopes of gradually taking over the women's work of the church.[22] The themes of its general conferences were also churchly rather than domestic,[23] as was the reordering and rewording of the original objectives in the 1960s.[24] Articles in the *South India Churchman* suggested that its leadership was seeking the partnership of men and women in the church.[25] Nevertheless, the fellowship was prevented by its limited resources and its constitution from becoming an independent body within the church,[26] while its modest proposals for more than just a subordinate and dependent position within the church were rejected.[27]

In 1978 the Women's Fellowship reworked its earlier objectives and added two significant new ones, for a new group of four:

1. To unite members in prayer, service and witness; and help them grow in deeper spiritual life.
2. To uphold the sanctity of Christian marriage and the family life; and to help in the Christian nurture of children.
3. To train women for participation and leadership in the Church and community.
4. To serve the under-privileged, and to seek to promote justice for all.[28]

By the end of 1982 it seemed to be making more progress toward meeting its third than its fourth objective, yet it had too many member fellowships among the poor and in the villages to be considered totally elitist in orientation.

The original aim of the Order for Women was

> to provide a means whereby the Church may recognize the ministry of such women who are engaged in full time service of the Church, and who, regarding their service as part of a life-long vocation, desire to accept the obligations and discipline of such an Order in fellowship with other women.[29]

The sisters were commissioned by diocesan bishops after approval by both the bishop and the Order. They placed themselves at the disposal of the church, working where the dioceses told them to work under service conditions set by the dioceses. What held them together was their common rule and their biannual retreat at the mother house in Bangalore. They experienced great difficulty recruiting new members because parents felt that doing whatever the church called upon them to do offered women less financial security than marriage did.[30]

By the mid-1960s the sisters had become concerned about their place in the church. In 1968 the Synod, "the supreme governing and legislative body of the Church of South India,"[31] referred the question of the role of the Order within the church to its Theological Commission, asking for, among other things, a clearer definition of the Order's position, function, and status as a lay or clerical body. In response the commission affirmed that "the Church should work towards a relationship of equality of men and women in the total life, work and witness of the church" and recommended that "the Synod and the Diocese should find ways of giving adequate security of service to women who offer themselves for full-time work in the Church" as well as that the relationship between the members of the Order and each diocese where they work shall be clarified.[32] Nonetheless, the Order's numbers remained small, and the number and proportion of full-time women workers in the Church of South India began to decline sharply (see Table I). In 1980 the Synod classified members of the Order with the clergy.

This marked the beginning of the Synod's direct involvement with issues surrounding the place and role of women in the church. In 1970 it endorsed the Theological Commission's views on the role of women in general and the Order for Women in particular, approved the commission's recommendation to ordain women as deacons subject to the same conditions as pertained to men, and referred to its Ministerial Committee an application from the Madras Diocese for the ordination of a woman as presbyter.[33] The ordination of women now became the major women's issue before the Synod.

The Synod's Ministerial Committee recommended ordination in 1972,

Year	Representation of Women at Synod Meetings			Women Members of the Synod Executive		Indian Women Full-Time Paid Evangelistic Workers (FPWs)[a]	
	Elected Delegates	Women as % of All Elected Lay Delegates	Women as % of Total Voting Delegates	Members	Substitutes	No. of Women FPWs	Women as % of Total FPWs
1948	17	18.5	9.8	1	0	—	—
1950	20	19.0	10.5	0	1	—	—
1952	24	27.3	13.6	1	1	—	—
1954	22	22.7	12.3[b]	0	1	1132	31.3
1956	27	27.8	14.3	2	0	1132	31.3
1958	23	23.7	12.4	2	1	1151	34.8
1960	26	24.5	13.1	1	0	1038	33.6
1962	31	30.4	15.5	2	1	921	34.3
1964	23	23.0	11.8	0	0	834	37.3
1966	20	19.2	9.9	1	0	686	34.4
1968	20	19.2	10.4	2	0	858[c]	36.8
1970	20	18.2	9.5	2	2	949	34.2
1972	13	11.6	6.2	1	0	577	28.2
1974	17	14.7	7.8	1	2	455	24.3
1976	15	12.6	7.9	1	2	447	27.7
1978	23	17.4	9.4	1	4	224	15.9
1980	29	19.9	11.0	1	1	281	17.9[d]
1982	22	16.7	8.2	0	3	236	16.4

Table I. Some Indices of Women's Participation as Decision Makers and Full-Time Paid Workers in the Church of South India, 1948–1982

a. This was a category of lay workers and does not include the ordained clergy.

b. From this time on, a maximum of ten delegates could be nominated by the Moderator. Except in 1982 at least one of these was a woman.

c. In this year the category was changed to "Lay Evangelistic or Pastoral Workers."

d. In this year the members of the Order for Women of the Church of South India were included among the ordained clergy. Had they continued in this category, they would have raised the percentages for 1980 and 1982 to 19.7% and 18.6%, respectively.

but the Synod accepted a Reference Committee ruling that the sentence in the constitution that reads "Men shall be ordained as presbyters in the Church of South India" referred only to males (that is, "men" was *not* being used here in the generic sense, although it is used generically elsewhere in the constitution).[34] Thus the ordination of women as presbyters (but not as deacons) required a constitutional amendment before it could become law. In 1974 a quorum was not present when the matter was to be voted upon. In 1975 the Theological Commission published a statement recommending women's ordination unanimously, providing biblical and theological arguments stressing the equality of the sexes and both affirming and denying common assumptions about the Indian woman. On the one hand, the commission pointed out that ordination cannot be withheld when there was "a new understanding of the dignity of womanhood" in India and when Indian women were being liberated from "age-long male domination," and that there were some aspects of the pastoral ministry (e.g., among children and other women) "for which qualified women pastors are better suited."[35] On the other hand, the commission rejected the views that women are impure because "divinely instituted biological processes" do not make a person unclean or unholy; that women are psychologically unfit because "men are also subject to psychological pressures and instability"; and that marriage is a disqualification, because marriage no more disqualifies women than men from ordination.[36]

The 1976 Synod, on recommendation from its Executive Committee, accepted the amendment "Men and women will be ordained as presbyters" with only one dissenting vote.[37] The General Secretary reported to the 1978 Synod that nine dioceses had voted in favor, six against, and four had not voted on the amendment. Consequently, the amendment did not yet have the necessary approval of two thirds of the dioceses. The Synod then accepted the Reference Committee ruling that because the time given to vote on amendments was the two years between Synods, this amendment was not accepted.[38] In 1980 the amendment was again presented to and accepted by the Synod, 215 to 9, and referred to the dioceses.[39] In 1982, unlike in 1978, the Synod declared that there was no time limit on the ratification of amendments, and so this one would go into effect when two thirds of the dioceses approved it,[40] which happened later that year.

Representation in the decision-making bodies of the church was the other major women's issue to come before the Synod in the 1970s. At no Synod meeting from 1948 to 1982 were women more than 30.4 percent of the elected lay delegates or 15.5 percent of the total voting delegates. Percentages of women delegates were higher in the early years of the Church of South India, when foreign missionary women still occupied positions of leadership, but have been consistently below the mean (20.4% and 10.8%) from the mid-1960s on. There has been an average of one woman and never more than two women on the forty- to sixty-member Synod Executive Committee. (See Table I.)

In 1976 the Synod passed resolutions making "a general policy that, wherever possible, in all Committees, Commissions and Councils of the C.S.I. Dioceses and Synod not less than 25% membership shall be women" and encouraging the dioceses to have women take a more active role in the preaching ministry, Sunday worship, and the pastoral minis- try at the local level.[41] Ironically, this same Synod approved an Executive Committee with no women on it save the General Secretary, who was an ex-officio member anyway. The 1978 Synod considered but did not approve a recommendation of the Women's Fellowship that its General Secretary be an ex-officio member of the Synod Executive Committee.[42] In 1980 she was made an Accredited Visitor to the Synod and its Execu- tive Committee.[43] In 1982 the Women's Fellowship made some specific recommendations to help assure better representation of women in deci- sion-making bodies, but their report was merely "received with apprecia- tion" and the Nominating Committee did not give them the 30 percent representation on Synod committees they had asked for.[44]

That the ordination and equal representation questions raised some larger issues for Indian women is apparent from the articles they wrote during the 1970s for the *South India Churchman.* Sister Elizabeth Paul argued that since the Indian woman's situation was changing, it was wrong to "determine what a woman is because of what she has been" and her customary practice of limiting herself to indirect influence upon the councils of the church through her husband or sons is power without responsibility.[45] Clara Clarke considered the Indian woman now a person in her own right, capable of shouldering responsibilities in church and society.[46] Daisy Gopal Ratnam urged women to consider themselves equal to men.[47] Others testified to women breaking old bonds, moving out of the home, acquiring new experience and new self-images to match. There was also, however, much exhortation of women by women, thus suggesting that many Indian Christian women had yet to experience the new realities which the authors described.

This brief survey suggests that the Church of South India exhibited throughout the period under study considerable continuity in its assump- tions about the Indian woman. Not only has its attention remained focused upon the Christian woman, and especially the educated Chris- tian woman, but it has also remained institutionally, and to only a slightly lesser degree ideologically, committed to the view that the Indian woman functions in a sphere separate from and subordinate to that of the Indian man. The Women's Fellowship, the Order for Women, and the separation of women's work from men's work, in all of which women do enjoy considerable autonomy but have not been allowed to be independent of male authority, have been expressions of this commitment.

Because of the separate spheres and the habit of mind it creates, the Indian woman has been quite invisible to the male-dominated church. From the negotiations leading to union through a conference with representatives of overseas churches on "Priorities for the Mission of the Church" in late 1981,[48] one confronts an extraordinary silence about women, partly because the church had other urgent matters to deal with (church union, redefining relationships with overseas churches, relating to a newly independent and democratic India as a religious minority), partly no doubt because men make more noise than women in the councils of the church, but partly also because women have really been considered to be of the *bene esse* rather than of the *esse* of the church. It is on this last point, of course, that the assumptions of women and men have diverged most sharply.

The other assumption that became both prominent and problematical in the 1970s was that the Indian woman is changing. This was a frequent argument for giving her a larger role in the church. Yet both men and women saw the Indian woman primarily as a family member, usually a wife-mother. As evidence of change among educated women began to mount in the early 1970s, articles appeared in the *South India Churchman* suggesting that the nature of the Christian home and the woman's role there was becoming a problem,[49] while even the staunchest advocates of the equality of the sexes stressed the importance of particularly the woman to the home.[50] The members of the Order for Women were, of course, exceptions to this rule; yet by putting themselves totally at the disposal of the church, even they accepted the submissive and self-sacrificing role of the traditional Indian wifely ideal.

God intends the Indian woman to continue to be a good Christian homemaker and to contribute to the upbuilding of the church. Moreover, the Church of South India has stated officially that the woman is an equal partner to man in creation, redemption, and calling to ministry and mission as part of the church. Every place in the church where men are is therefore now a proper place for the Indian woman also: the ordained ministry including the episcopacy, decision-making bodies at all levels, in all aspects of ministry and mission. Her role is to be in these places, contributing her special gifts and going where and doing what only she as a woman can go or do. However, there is a large gap between the church's proclamation and its performance in this respect, thus suggesting that the changes are greater in what is permitted women, in what the

rules allow her to do and to be, than in the church's actual working
assumptions.

IV

In 1947 when India became independent and the Church of South
India was born, the Indian woman was a priority concern neither for the
church nor for the state. The state assumed some responsibility for her
welfare but did not treat her as a significant contributor to national
development. The Protestant churches acted on similar assumptions.
When these churches were developing new structures more suitable to
their new circumstances and redefining relationships with foreign missions, the place of the Indian woman in the new order came as something
of an afterthought. Then, acting on welfare rather than development
assumptions, the churches assigned her to a separate, subordinate, and
restricted sphere within their ministry and mission. Both appeals for
partnership and the efforts of women, who found this arrangement
confining and essentially unchristian, to use what autonomy they enjoyed
to enlarge the woman's sphere within the church's life and work during
the 1950s and 1960s must be seen in this context.

In the 1970s a growing body of educated Protestant women, now with
Indian rather than foreign missionary spokespersons, began to challenge
this arrangement both theologically and politically. The NCCI publications indicate that some of these women were moving in outward-look-
ing, liberationist directions, while the CSI sources indicate that others
were seeking larger, more equal roles for women within the structures
of the churches. Although the assumptions about the Indian woman of
the former were mass-oriented and negative in their assessments of past
change, whereas those of the latter tended to be more elitist and positive,
neither held up the liberated Western woman as a model to emulate and
both shared a basically sociological rather than psychological mode of
thinking about the Indian woman. Both invariably described what constitutes or ought to constitute the feminine in terms of the roles women
play and the skills they acquire in the process, and only rarely in terms
of what the Indian woman's essential nature or distinctive psychology
is.[51]

This common mode of thinking about women, the changing and varying assumptions about the Indian woman on which Protestants based
church policies and programs affecting women, as well as the nature and
timing of the challenges to and/or changes in those policies and programs all indicate that the Protestant churches were arenas in which the
post-Independence women's movement occurred. Other studies of Indian women have shown how basically Indian are both the specific

assumptions described in this chapter and the sociological mode of thinking about the Indian woman.[52] Patricia Caplan's insight that Indian women's organizations tend to function as extensions of their domestic roles applied as much to Protestant women's fellowships as to those associations in Madras she described in 1978.[53] Indeed, studies of women and family social customs in Kerala, the dowry problem in the city of Bangalore, and the attitude survey covering the whole of India in *Towards Equality* all show how little Christians differ from other Indians in their attitudes and behavior toward women.[54] Finally, the basic trends in the Indian women's movement since 1947 have been replicated in the Protestant churches with striking faithfulness. In the 1970s there were clear signs that Protestant women had entered the third phase of the women's movement, albeit like most others in limited ways. They were challenging the patriarchal assumptions of church policymakers; they were reaching out to less privileged women within and outside the churches as part of a common struggle for justice; they were aware of and participating in the activities of nonchurch women's groups.[55]

However, they differed from other Indians facing similar obstacles and seeking similar objectives on at least two points, and it is here that their distinctiveness within the Indian context lies. They made extensive use of the Bible, and especially of Jesus' treatment of women, for guidance in understanding what God intended the Indian woman to become and what therefore her place in the church ought to be. Of special significance in this regard was the widely used Bible study booklet, *Good News for Women,* first published in 1979 and subsequently translated into at least five Indian languages.[56] But whether a common Christian faith actually succeeded in uniting women across class lines in a common pursuit of what God intended them to become cannot be discerned from the sources consulted. In addition, among India's many religious communities and organizations, only in the Protestant churches has the ordination of women to the priesthood been a major women's issue. The significance of this issue cannot be overemphasized, not just because it symbolized an equality of the sexes but—what is more important—because it constituted a profound rejection of traditional Indian sentiments with regard to the ritual impurity of women.

II
THE ROLE OF WOMEN
IN THE CHURCH

3

Sor Juana Inés de la Cruz: The First Woman Theologian in the Americas

Beatriz Melano Couch

S or Juana Inés de la Cruz (1651–1695) was both a mystic and the first woman theologian in the Americas, North and South. This fact has gone unrecognized by scholars, who nonetheless have considered her to be one of the most brilliant and creative literary figures of her time, and even of Spanish culture.[1] This chapter is divided into two parts. The first, based on an autobiographical letter that is at the same time an apologia for her vocation as a scholar and writer, provides a brief biography of this extraordinary woman. The second provides the basis of her claim to be a theologian.

I

Sor Juana was born on November 12, 1651, in a small village of the Mexican region of Amecameca, seventy kilometers to the southeast of Mexico City. Her father, Pedro Manuel de Asbaje y Vargas, was a native of the Basque region of Spain, and her mother, Isabel Ramírez de Santillana, was Mexican born. We know that Sor Juana had three sisters and three half-brothers and that her mother at the end of her life declared herself "single," making Juana de Asbaje what then was called "a natural child," a child born out of wedlock.

In a letter dated March 1, 1691, and sent to Father Manuel Fernandez de Santa Cruz, the Bishop of Puebla—although addressed to a pseudonymous "Sor Filotea" because a nun could not write to a man in those times —Sor Juana defended herself against the accusations of not having enough dedication to her duties as a religious woman and dedicating too much time to "profane literature" by providing the following information about her life. She stated that at age three she already knew how to read; at six or seven she heard about the University of Mexico and

wanted to attend dressed as a man, since women were not then accepted
for studies. She read tirelessly in those years, even though she was
punished for doing so, and wrote "Loa Eucharistica," a theological poem
that has been lost. When nine years old, while staying in the home of
relatives in Mexico City, she learned Latin in nine lessons. Her desire for
knowledge was insatiable. At the age of fifteen, in the court of the viceroy
Mancera, where she had been received two years earlier, she was examined before forty doctors of all the sciences of the time and passed with
a signal triumph.

   In 1667 she entered a convent of the Barefoot Carmelites but left it
three months later because she had so little time for study there. Then
in 1669, when she was eighteen, she entered the Convent of Saint Jerome,
where she worked as an accountant and file clerk but spent most of her
time studying and writing. She came to have one of the largest libraries
of her time, with works in Latin, Greek, Portuguese, and Spanish. She
claimed that her inclination to study was born of God but cost her, in
her own words, "hate, malevolence, persecution, and suffering."[2] She
compared her experience with the furious hatred of the Pharisees for
Christ, saying that she suffered a great deal as a target of envy because
of her pursuit of knowledge and her vocation as theologian and writer.
To quote her letter, "There was a rouse of emulations and persecutions,
so many that I cannot even count. . . . I have been persecuted for my
love of wisdom and literature, not because I had reached one or the
other. . . . I have been persecuted through hate and malevolence."[3] When
her superiors finally prohibited her from studying at all, she replied that
such a measure was clearly one fully in the style of the Inquisition. She
actually went even further in her own defense, affirming something
entirely unheard of in her day: namely, the right of women in general
to have access to training. In order to support her position she made
careful use of historical, ecclesiastical, and theological material, arriving
thus at an astonishingly broad view of the role of women in society, in
learning, and, above all, in the church. Not only did she know the Bible,
the church fathers, history, mythology, and literature, but also all the
sciences of her day. She was surely in every way, except in actually
having the label used for her, a feminist. To quote her: "God gives talent
for sacred use and it is so unjust that not only women (considered inept)
but also men (who, simply by being thus, consider themselves wise) are
forbidden the interpretation of the Holy Scriptures if they are not erudite
and virtuous."[4] For Sor Juana the lack of wisdom (meaning the denial
of access to learning) was heresy, and she denounced the greed and
vanity of many who wrote without having talent. She proclaimed with
audacity the liberty of women, quoting great women saints such as
Theresa of the Child Jesus or Theresa of Avila.

Her greatest aspiration was to study theology, prohibited for the women of her age, and she translated all of Jerome's works from Latin into Spanish. In order to have access to theology, one had to climb the steps of other sciences and human arts, and for that reason she studied logic, rhetoric, physics, music, arithmetic, geometry, architecture, history, and law. With much humility she remarked, "I have studied all these things and I know nothing."[5] She also defended writing poetry as a way of serving God, since she had been accused of not carrying through a life of contemplation because of her dedication to poetry. After citing the psalms, the prophets, and the songs of the Old and New Testaments, she asked, "What is wrong about my writing them too?"[6]

In 1691 and 1692 there were in Mexico many crises produced by wheat blight, bad harvests, fires, hunger, theft, assaults, and rebellions. During those years Sor Juana lived more in the convent and less "in the world." As one of her commentators has said, she began on *the road of silence,*

> each day less dedicated to books and more dedicated to charity; every time less given to scientific experiments and more drawn by spiritual exercises. Her confessor says: "She does not run in virtue but flies." Silences, devotions, little writing; silences which will last till the 17th of April 1695, when she succumbed to the plague which was overtaking the convent of Saint Jerome.[7]

During this period Sor Juana underwent a spiritual change that revealed a nearly exclusive dedication to contemplative life and service. In 1693, when she was forty-two years of age, she ceased writing philosophical, theological, and literary works. It is probably a valid hypothesis that at this time she also gave away her library of 4,000 volumes and all her scientific instruments, especially those she used to study astronomy.

There is in the Book of Professions *(Libro de Profesiones)* of the Convent of Saint Jerome (signed in February 1694) an interesting and significant document, maybe the last document of Sor Juana. It reveals her mystical attitude and complete self-surrender into the hands of God, as well as of the church, with a deep sense of God's will and justice. There she reaffirmed her vows as a religious person or, as she said, made a "renewal of her vows," and there is also what we may call both a reaffirmation of God's final judgment and her submission to it, as well as a prayer of confession of sins and a statement of faith in forgiveness and grace. It is possible to date this "mystical" petition to March 1694.[8] There is in it a clear sense of seriousness, a clear and recognizable baroque literary style, a wealth of suggestive references to the intellect, a warm humor, a moving sense of sorrow, a deep feeling of freedom.

Free as she was and possessed of the knowledge that the soul is the constructor of its own prisons and its own free open spaces, Sor Juana wanted to surrender totally to her vocation. For her the greatest "goodness" was to die freely surrendered to her own condition, bonded to the mystical body of Christ. Sor Juana set herself squarely before the gaze of the living God and harvested from that a wisdom expressed in some of her lines of poetry.

> To see men's hearts
> One need not understand them
> Because for Thee they are evident,
> for Thee, the inmost recess of the Abysm.

In 1689 Sor Juana's complete works were published in Madrid and in the following year, in Mexico. In 1691 not only did her theological work entitled *Letter (or Answer) to Sor Filotea de la Cruz* appear but also the first volume of her *Complete Works* was reedited in Barcelona. She died among the sisters of the convent of San Jerónimo on April 17, 1695.

"One has to imagine Sor Juana, in her early death, seeing the world illuminated that looks at her, . . . awake to the spirit."[9]

II

Scholars who have studied Sor Juana speak of her greatness as a literary figure, philosopher, and woman of science. My study of her works has brought me to the conclusion that she was also a theologian: indeed, the first woman theologian in all the Americas. Sor Juana's theological vocation is exceptionally clear, especially in an age when *any* vocation was suspect if pursued by a woman, in such writings of hers as the *Athenagoric Letter* (also known as *Crisis of a Sermon*), in much of her poetry and other writings of less significance, and in some sections of her autobiography in the *Letter to Sor Filotea de la Cruz.*

The elaborate thesis of Antonio Vieira was based on the affirmation that the most notable greatness of Christ was to become absent, not to die: that is to say, the greatest "goodness" of Christ lay in the fact that he "disappeared" from the world for a particular time, the time between his death and resurrection. Sor Juana took issue with this, using the theology of Augustine and the holy scriptures as the basis for her argument and affirming that Christ's most notable greatness was to die for us. She also stated that even during the three days of his descent into hell he was present in the sacrament, which makes him, precisely, present. The theological theses of Sor Juana were indeed distinctly accurate, as can be seen in the relevant sections of the Spanish text of her *Carta Atenagórica* (here in my translation).

I feel with Saint Augustine that the greatness and goodness of Christ was to die. This is proved because the most valuable [gift] that a man has is his life and dignity and both things Christ gives up in his ignominious death. According to God's part, he had already done to man the greatest goodness worthy of his omnipotence such as creating, conserving him, etc., but as man [Christ as God and fully human] he has nothing more he could give than [his] life. . . . Christ says, "Remember that I have died." He does not say, "Remember that I created you, that I became incarnated, that I became sacramented, etc." Therefore the greatest thing is to die. . . . Moreover, the other goodnesses of Christ are referred to but they are not represented. Death is referred to, it is recommended, and it is represented. Therefore not only is it the greatest goodness but it is the summary of all the other goodnesses. I will prove it. Christ through his death repeats to us the benefit of creation because he restores through [his death] the primitive [human] being of grace.[10] Christ through his death gives us again [the benefit] of conservation, because he does not only conserve for us the temporal life, dying that we may live, but he also gives to us his flesh and blood as sustenance. Christ through his death reiterates for us the benefit of the incarnation because, uniting us in the incarnation to the purest flesh of his mother, in his death he unites himself with all of us, shedding his blood for all of us. Only the sacrament seems not to be represented during his death, and that is because the sacrament is the representation of his death. And this in itself proves that the greatest goodness was his death: because the sacrament being such a great goodness, it is only the representation of the death.[11] . . . In truth till now we have not answered the author; we have defended only the feelings [the theological position] of Augustine. . . . Let us treat the first [issue], that is to prove that Christ did not absent himself. His own argument will serve as a proof for mine [my own argument]. It is said [Antonio Vieira's thesis] that Christ suffers so much his making himself absent and so little the death, that he delays the remedy of the death in the resurrection till the third day and anticipates the fact of his absence in the sacrament. Why did he sweat in the garden: *factus est sudor eius?* Why did he agonize out of grief: *factus in agonia?* How is it that he makes himself absent, if he remains present in the sacrament in the upper room? And if he remedies the absence before it takes place, what is the absence he feels, when he has already overcome it? Therefore the agony cannot be because he departs if he has already assured his presence. Moreover, from all of this one infers that making himself absent cannot be taken to be the greatest goodness of Christ, and not even as goodness because he really never did it. . . . Furthermore, the absent one feels only the actual fact of not seeing what he loves . . . the one who dies or sees dying feels the lack and feels the death of his beloved one or feels the lack of the presence of the beloved and his own death. Therefore death is more painful than absence, because absence is only absence; death is death and absence. Therefore if one understands it in depth, all the more painful it will be.[12]

From these fragments we can deduce that she not only had a keen intelligence and an ability to reason clearly but also had theological insight. The subject matter of this debate with Father Antonio Vieira may not be relevant to a twentieth-century audience, but we must recognize that Sor Juana had the freedom and audacity to debate on equal terms with a male theologian, something unheard of at that time. Women in general, and religious women in particular, not only did not have access to theological and secular circles of investigation but also would rarely have dared enter into debate with their male colleagues. Indeed, as mentioned in the previous section, in her *Letter to Sor Filotea de la Cruz,* Sor Juana defends the right of all women, and especially of religious women, to have access to learning and to use it, in whatever form they chose, in the service of Christ and of the church. She stated, using Paul and Eusebius as foundations, that women were teachers and prophets. She also affirmed the necessity of knowing the history, customs, and ceremonies of each era in order to interpret the scriptures faithfully— a clearly modern view that one would not expect in the writings of a woman theologian of three centuries ago.[13]

The *Primer Sueño* (a long poem) of Sor Juana has been studied by great literary critics as a masterful piéce of baroque literature and philosophy,[14] but I find that it is also a theological work, since it is in its essence a work in which truth is searched out. For Sor Juana truth is to be found in God, and more specifically in Jesus Christ, even though she used pagan mythology throughout as an appropriately baroque symbolic language to refer to philosophical and theological truth. There is a series of symbols that represent the world of darkness and of light in a dialectic between day and night, light and darkness, body and soul, sleeping and waking. All this symbolism points to the eruption of truth, and thus the world comes to be illuminated by the light, which is God, symbolized by the sun. Thus the self is awakened, having arrived at knowledge. Night is ambiguous and symbolizes negative forces. It is a purging symbol. Light, on the other hand, is interpreted as the possibility of knowledge, which is not immediate, but rather takes an intellectual, Aristotelian form, perhaps closer to a discerning of Being, although rationally limited.

Sor Juana denied the possibility of a total and immediate knowledge as well as of a final and absolute knowledge, a possibility that some theologians in her era affirmed. In this fundamental philosophical and theological affirmation, Sor Juana precedes what modern philosophers call "the school of suspicion": that is to say, those thinkers who affirm that after Freud and Nietzsche immediate and trustworthy knowledge of full truth and reality through either rational or intuitive means is considered impossible. This apparent skepticism is a way of describing the finitude of human rationality and, why not, as José Gaos suggests, the encounter of faith?[15]

Another thesis I venture to put forward is that Sor Juana was a mystic, although her literary critics either question or deny this, insisting that she did not enter into a contemplative life but, rather, took up rational thought and the writing of literary and philosophical works. Nevertheless, a mystic, in the original sense of the term, was a person dedicated to the spiritual life and to the knowledge of God through immediate experience; later, "mystic" meant a person whose knowledge of God was accompanied by revelations and states of ecstasy. In the case of Sor Juana, as far as is known, there was neither ecstasy nor revelation, but there was indeed a spiritual and contemplative life of definite depth, of rational knowledge but under the direction of the Spirit. Thus Sor Juana was a mystic. Deep and direct experience of God himself was an essential part of her life and work and became most apparent in the final years of her life, as indicated earlier.

It has not been my purpose to make a detailed philosophical and theological analysis of all of Sor Juana's works, for that would require more than a short essay. What has been said serves to introduce a great woman, who was the first woman theologian in Latin America and on the whole American continent—and that in the seventeenth century, one of the least promising times and places for such excellence and contemporaneity.

4

Coming of Age
in a Latin Church

Katherine Gilfeather, M.M.

Reminiscent, perhaps, of a less complex reality, the title "Coming of Age in a Latin Church" is nonetheless peculiarly apt. Adolescents emerging from the shadow-world bridging childhood and adult life weave awkwardly out of the dimness, where they were "seen but not heard," into the disconcerting daylight of public acceptance of their right to exercise responsible decisions. A striking similarity can be drawn between this coming of age in society and the present stage in the metamorphosis of woman's role within the Catholic Church. Although all comparisons limp, the essential is here retained; from a fundamentally passive role within church structures, women are moving toward adult responsibility for the church's life and worship.

However, the move could hardly be described as carefully orchestrated. Neither uniform nor universal, woman's coming of age in the church is proving to be as "stormy"[1] as that of the emerging adolescent. This is due in part to the fact that the role change is not coming about in *a* church, but within any number of churches; not within a monolithic structure, but within the vast range of cultures and subcultures in which women live and worship in union with Rome. Molded, enriched, or impoverished by its past, and immersed in its contemporary struggles, the local or national church—the term is used to refer to the Catholic Church in Chile under the guidance of its Conference of Bishops—will tend to view all reality and discover its pastoral priorities, roles, and functions through the relative power or distortion of its own peculiar optic.

Clearly, the role of women within this ecclesial melange will vary considerably from local church to local church; hence the need to consider each in depth and thereby avoid generalizations. This chapter is devoted to a descriptive analysis of the role of women—both lay and religious—within the Catholic Church in Chile over the past seventeen years. The results of four studies spanning the years from 1966 to 1983 will form the basis for our comments and provide the itinerary for what has been a fascinating journey.

A Call to Change: Conciliar and Preconciliar Stirrings

In 1961–62, even before Vatican II, the Chilean Episcopate had begun to meet with experts and technicians in the elaboration of a Pastoral Plan for the country. This plan was to initiate a series of changes that even the bishops themselves could not have foreseen.

Lamenting the lack of a global plan for pastoral action or evangelization, the document underscored the ignorance and divorce from reality that was endemic within the church at that time, insisting that "the objective of the apostolate of the Church is man and that this man lives in the world by the will of God and for this reason must dedicate himself to the world."[2] The document stressed the need for penetrating the world, above all the most abandoned sectors. This penetration was seen to require a direct confrontation with socioeconomic problems, if the church was serious about giving preference to the laboring class.

The plan included a general mission for the entire country during 1963. Called the "Gran Misión," it reached the most distant corners of the land and the most abandoned of its people through the recruiting of hundreds of women religious—hereafter referred to as sisters—seminarians, priests, and dedicated laity. An unanticipated consequence of this process was the conscientization of great numbers of sisters for whom a hitherto unknown world had been opened. The great majority, dedicated to education and largely unaware of the problems of pastoral work among the poor, now found themselves changed by their experience and, in some cases, convinced of a new direction in their lives.

Then in its third session (1964), the Second Vatican Council was having its own major impact. The council fathers had stated firmly that in the gospel and in the tradition of the church "the poor" occupied a place of preference with respect to the announcement of the message of salvation. Early conciliar texts were received with enthusiasm and widely promulgated. Study and reflection on them became common during those years, and many sisters had their own copies of the documents and used them for private reading and meditation.

It was during those halcyon years subsequent to the council that an in-depth study of sisters was initiated in Santiago.[3] When the sample was set up in 1966, it was found that, of the more than 150 active congregations of sisters in Chile at that time, more than 75 percent were involved in education. Small numbers were to be found in health-related ministries and catechetical programs. We became particularly interested in educators, both for the richness and variety the sample might offer and for their key position in the formation of youth. The educational level of these women was normally higher than that of other sisters, and one would expect, as a consequence, that their consciousness and openness would be on a par with their academic preparation. Living in the capital, they were likewise at the heart of renewal in the church and its earliest efforts at implementation of council decrees.

With all this in mind, an interview questionnaire of 153 items was devised and a sampling of fifty congregations chosen, including 325 women, 63 percent of whom were under forty years of age. We have included the most pertinent findings in each of six areas of interest included in the survey.

1. *Consciousness of current problems on all levels*
   - 74% recognized that they knew almost nothing of what was going on in their provinces, municipalities, and neighborhoods
   - 66% declared that they knew little or nothing about the Pastoral Plan of their bishops, although theoretically the plan was to be the inspiration and substance of their own ministries (the plan had been in print and available for four years)
   - Almost 50% never read a newspaper and, among them, many were not even permitted to do so
2. *Relations with laity and those whose world views differed*
   - 40% expressed strong or potentially strong intolerance of the rights of non-Catholics or atheists to liberty of expression in a Catholic country
   - 32% felt that communication with others had nothing to do with our future happiness in heaven
   - 58% felt that priests and religious had received a higher call to holiness than the laity
3. *Attitudes toward work and personal ministry*
   - 43% felt the best contribution they could make to the solution of social problems was to pray about them
   - 30% felt that only the teaching of religion was directly apostolic
   - 36% declared that their personal sanctification ranked higher than any apostolic obligation; another 10% were undecided but leaned in the same direction
4. *Relations with students, parents, and neighbors*
   - 57% said they never visited the homes of students or ex-students—indeed, of anyone. Of this group, 40% were forbidden to do so by their own constitutions
   - 77% had little or no contact whatever with people living next door to their convents
   - 65% gave little or no time to conversation with their students outside the classroom

5. *The social dimension of evangelical poverty*
   - 31% affirmed that if a congregation were not founded explicitly to work with the poor, it had no obligation to do so; another 13% were indecisive or uninterested in the topic
   - Over 50% felt that the church's renewal had nothing whatsoever to do with the rejection of prestige, power, and wealth
6. *Position in the face of current changes in the church*
   - 49% saw the church in great danger because of too-rapid changes
   - 59% felt it important to teach that God was most pleased with unquestioned acceptance of one's socioeconomic position
   - 32% affirmed that private property rights surpassed in importance the common good; another 21% were unsure

Asked to delineate the prime factors influencing their decision to enter the novitiate, these women gave highest importance to the love of God, a sense of calling, and an attraction to religious life as a style of living. The least importance was attributed to a desire to serve the poor.

Although one is struck by the relatively large percentages of these women voicing preconciliar attitudes, it is also just as obvious that substantial groups were forging ahead against the rather serious threat of traditional structures, now no longer functional. Rereading the results of this investigation seventeen years later, one is struck by a sense of standing on the threshold of a new era. Walls were tumbling on all sides within the church, and freedom was in the air. Yes, there were hard questions, challenges to long-held assumptions, but we appeared to be on the way. Unfortunately, as the results of our research imply, many had a long way to go.

Vatican II, initiated in 1962, was to span a period of four years before its final session in 1965. Church leaders required four years of deliberation to achieve an unprecedented revision of the totality of the church's meaning and mission; it would take far longer for its members even to begin to comprehend the depth of the changes awaiting them. All too soon the first excitement of Vatican II began to fade into the hard reality of implementation. It was not enough to read and discuss council documents and attend endless workshops; the documents were basically a call to conversion, and conversion has always meant painful change. It was in 1968 that the Latin-American Conference of Bishops met together with theologians and social scientists in Medellín, Colombia, for reflection and analysis of the council documents in light of the devastating reality of their continent. This was the genesis of the Medellín Documents (1969), which were destined to grip the minds and hearts of Christians throughout Latin America and, indeed, the world.

Women in Ministry: A Dwindling Clergy

One of the more serious unanticipated consequences of the council and its disquieting reverberations throughout the church was an unprecedented loss of religious personnel. Large numbers of women left their congregations and scores of clerics sought freedom from the obligations of their priesthood. Although the phenomenon was universal, the resulting pastoral dilemma was especially grave in those areas in which priests were already too few and in which vocations never permitted an adequate response to pastoral problems. During the 1970s there was approximately one priest for every 800 baptized Catholics in the United States; in Chile we could count on one for every 4,000. With the aftermath of the council even this was utopian. Long plagued by a dwindling clergy and a perennial lack of sufficient funding for its activities, the Chilean church had been forced to seek alternatives to normal pastoral procedures by developing creative solutions to problems. We were to see concrete evidence of that creativity in the pastoral action of the church subsequent to Vatican II.

In early 1970 a catechetical program initiated in the capital, Santiago, soon spread throughout the remaining dioceses. Called "Mamás Catequistas" (Mother Catechists), the program trained mothers to teach religion to their own and other children at home. Christian formation was literally returned to the hearth, and laywomen were doing it. Five years later at least 10,000 women were participating in the program in Santiago alone. At the same time, sisters in a few rural parishes without resident priests were named administrators. They took over those tasks traditionally reserved to clergy: planning and conducting paraliturgical ceremonies and carrying the entire burden of religious formation of adults and children—prebaptismal talks for parents, prematrimonial formation for couples, the formation of basic communities for Christian living, parochial administration, and a limited participation in the administration of the sacraments. By 1976 there were nearly 80 of these "sister administrators" in parishes all over Chile. A small but significant number of other sisters left their larger convents to live in low-income housing in marginal areas, identifying as much as possible with the people. Their groups were small, their lives simple, their goal to support themselves.

Women, lay and religious, became moderators of Centers for Mothers in marginal areas, giving courses in leadership training, conducting reflection groups, and helping women to form neighborhood associations as a basis for solidarity. When the problem of hunger became so explicit after 1973, the church attempted to address it through its "dining rooms" for younger children, where thousands received one meal daily.

By 1976 there were 320 of these projects throughout the Santiago area alone, all under the responsibility of local women who prepared meals, served the children, and often begged for the contents of the following day's fare at the itinerant markets dotting the city.

Women were apparently becoming accustomed to taking pastoral responsibility and were encouraged to do so. They were everywhere in the church, or almost everywhere. It was the "almost" that led many to formulate a series of questions with respect to this massive incorporation of women into the pastoral action of the church. Why was such importance being given to their incorporation? Was there something that could not be accomplished without woman's participation? Was the advancement of Catholic women in Chile indicative of their evermore decisive position in institutions and structures of the church? Was the advancement the result of deliberate planning, or on the contrary, was it a case of merely "filling in," a temporary solution to the priest shortage of a particular historical moment? The answers to these questions were of some importance, since they would affect the mode of participation and the level of authority that women would eventually attain.

How Women Were Seen by Ecclesial Authority

In 1975 a study of the Chilean episcopacy was initiated,[4] and we were able to include questions bearing on this theme of pastoral promotion of women. Thirty bishops were asked to give their reasons for the expansion of activities for women within the church, which activities should remain outside their domain and why, and whether or not such expansion was in fact beneficial to the church.

Asked why they felt women had extended their field of action in the church, 47 percent responded in terms of "women's peculiarly feminine qualities": for example, devotion, diligence, constancy, self-sacrifice, generosity, docility. The church was seen by 27 percent as a unique "locus" in which God is acting to promote women in a special way. A similar group saw the phenomenon as the result of action on the part of women who were extending the scope of their responsibility to all areas of society. Fifty-seven percent of these bishops thought that this growing participation was generally beneficial, but for more than a third of this same group the response "yes but" showed deep concern over the possible danger of feminizing the church to such an extent that men would feel alienated—a perennial danger facing the church in Chile.

When asked to express their views with regard to women in specific areas of pastoral work, only 7 percent of the bishops felt that all pastoral tasks were as equally open to women as to men. Ninety percent declared Major Orders (priesthood) for women impossible and beyond discussion;

43 percent excluded even preaching from consideration. Interestingly, some bishops opposed works in which women, particularly rural residents, were already involved; 17 percent refused to accept women as administrants of some sacraments, and 13 percent rejected their leadership in Christian communities that were without a priest. In expressing the reasons behind these stances, 33 percent based their rejection on the "machistic" culture of Chilean society and their related fears of alienating men by feminizing the church. In a society in which religion has traditionally been seen as "something for women," this is perhaps a real danger. Thirty percent gave the "tradition of the church" as basis for their viewpoint (e.g., "Christ selected only men for this role"). Almost 27 percent cited those "peculiarly feminine characteristics" as the principal reason for debarring women from priesthood. Strangely, "peculiarly feminine characteristics" were cited previously as reasons for the expansion of their participation. This time, however, the reference is to such traits as lack of maturity, a tendency to be led by sentiment and intuition rather than by reason and intelligence, a lack of experience and global vision, and delicacy. Reflection on the possibility of priesthood and preaching for women was considered premature and unnecessary by 20 percent, illegitimate by 23 percent, barbaric and infantile by 7 percent.

A pattern of attitudes can be discerned here that might be summarized as follows: The bishops of Chile, the religious authority of the church, have been hard pressed to solve their pastoral problems; women are proving a welcome addition to the task force. Their participation is highly limited, however, by the bishops' fear of feminizing the church, by reason of Chilean cultural traditions; their own attitudes toward women are symptomatic of the same traditions that have become determinants of the parameters of woman's pastoral participation and therefore of her participation in authority. At the same time, a pattern of positive qualities emerges, those considered "essentially feminine" by the hierarchy and ideally to be desired for all women: devotion, dedication, diligence, constancy, self-sacrifice, generosity, docility, piety, and affectivity.

How Chilean Women Saw Themselves

Although the values of the ecclesiastical structure are being transformed by historical necessity, there are cultural values, ideals, and norms that persist throughout society and create what appears to be a paradoxical situation. Because they are less tangible and unconscious, cultural values are transformed far more slowly and, for this reason, offer serious obstacles to any durable change in more visible structures. When a lack of coordination exists between structural and cultural changes, tensions, at times paradoxical, will appear and contrary attitudes will exist side by side.

This was in fact our initial prognosis initiating a study of women who were working within the Catholic Church in Santiago in 1975.[5] In taking stock of changes up to that date we perceived an ecclesiastical framework that had undergone structural and procedural changes under duress. Some of those changes had incorporated rather large numbers of women into pastoral action. However, the question was whether cultural attitudes had been changed or even touched in any parallel fashion.

The 202 women included in our sample enjoyed some degree of status in the local church; that is to say, they possessed a visible rank of some importance and real pastoral responsibility that enhanced and expanded their normal roles. Less than 25 percent of the sample were sisters; it was therefore a strongly lay-oriented group.

A comparison of the responses of these women with those of their bishops on similar topics offers a series of fascinating contrasts. In fact, the only areas of significant congruency could be found in their perceptions of "self-fulfillment" and of which traits were essentially feminine or masculine. Seventy-seven percent of these women felt themselves fulfilled by their labors for the church and defined that fulfillment in terms of "an opportunity to give myself in personal self-sacrifice." It is not surprising that more than 80 percent considered self-sacrifice to be essentially feminine, along with delicacy, prudence (48%), intuition (88%), and affectivity (71%).

Bishops tended to see the church as taking the initiative in promoting women, whereas women saw their promotion as the result of a historical necessity impelling the church. Whereas bishops showed themsleves to be defensive, intransigent, and impatient with the topics of ordination for women and women preachers, women based any opposition solely on lack of preparation, thereby indicating some openness to future possibilities.

Bishops tended to choose a church model with room for all levels of commitment and belonging that would at the same time maintain good relations with governments and avoid actions that would provoke restrictive measures. Women, on the other hand, chose a model with a reduced but highly committed membership, one that would take a more prophetic stance in the face of injustice.

The most urgent pastoral priority for the bishops was the lack of priestly vocations; the second was the need to augment pastoral personnel with dedicated laymen. The women gave as both first and second priorities "the need to build strong, effective Christian communities." The bishops were preoccupied with personnel—the means—whereas women tended to face the pastoral problem itself.

The bishops feared a feminization of the church and sought to curtail the parameters of their promotion, stopping short of certain symbolic roles. On the other hand the women were aware of their already-heavy burdens and responsibilities and did not equate responsibility with acquiring a particular role or status. For them it was an issue of real responsibility versus the symbol of office.

The foregoing offers some evidence of a positive relationship between rising status and changing religious ideology among these women. Above all, they were putting some distance between themselves and the cultural attitudes of their milieu. Sheer numbers offered a clear indication, moreover, that the supremacy of male influence in the pastoral area of the Chilean church was on the wane. Unplanned and apparently undesired by the incumbents, it was nonetheless a historical fact.

Women and the Poor: Innovative Ministry

Accepting the essential concepts of Vatican II and Medellín meant accepting the need for "change" as a constant in life. This required both elasticity to absorb changing circumstance and firmness to maintain a sense of continuity and essential integrity. The effort to achieve this balance had been costly for the church and its personnel. Faced with the necessity of making the good news understandable above all to the poor and marginated, they saw both that many church structures and methods had lost their meaning in the light of actual circumstances and that it was now the responsibility of pastoral agents, sisters and priests, to confront and solve pastoral dilemmas.

In our opinion it was the conjunction of Chilean Episcopal concern expressed in the Pastoral Plan,[6] the experience of the "Gran Misión" of 1963, and the strong impact of Vatican II that prepared the way for the first experiments with small communities of sisters in marginal areas of Santiago. Later the Medellín Documents[7] would lend further support to this innovation. There were clear indications that many religious congregations wished to commit themselves and their members to the needs of the poor and to reject former commitments to the dominant and favored minorities of society. It was just a beginning, but its real significance would be apparent only with the passage of time. It was a response to the challenge of Medellín to religious communities:

> The particular mandate of the Lord to evangelize the poor should bring us to a distribution of our resources and apostolic personnel in such a way that

effective preference is given to those sectors that are most in need, economically poor and segregated for whatever cause.[8]

In 1977, at the request of members of the Chilean hierarchy, Centro Bellarmino began a study of a group of sisters who had answered the call of Medellín in a concrete fashion. These women aspired to reach the marginal sectors of society through an innovative pastoral approach that allowed them a close identification with all aspects of that life-style. The changes and frustrations that this decision had brought about in their lives as well as in their attitudes toward the church and its structures were among the dimensions researched.

The Women and Their Environment

Limiting our sample to those women who were living and working in *poblaciones* (slums) throughout Santiago and various northern and southern provinces, we included sixty-one small communities of from two to three members, with a total of 136 interviews. Seventy-one percent of these women were from thirty to fifty years of age, a relatively young group, although not excessively so in light of the rigors of this style of life. Educational levels were high; almost 70 percent had either university degrees or normal school diplomas. The majority were foreigners with less than ten years in the country. More than 90 percent were living in marginal areas by their own choice and not as the result of an assignment.

To attempt to describe a *población* adequately would require more space than this chapter allows. Suffice it to say that conditions are harsh and totally foreign for those from a middle-class background. This was the case for the majority of our sample. Imagine tiny, cramped quarters, cheap cane furniture, flower pots to replace gardens, unpaved streets and their fine sea of dust that fills the air and covers everything in summer only to become a morass of mud and puddles during the rainy cold winter. Add poor sanitation, inadequate heating, lack of privacy, high noise level (radios playing incessantly at full volume, the crying and screams of children), the ever-present *cantinas* (bars) and their drunken clientele, overcrowding, undernourishment, unemployment, the sick, the old, the dying—and in it all—not having the means to change much of anything.

This preoccupation with the human condition, with suffering and despair, had its impact upon those women who chose to identify with this sector of society. It was precisely this impact that we chose to probe in an effort to assess the effects of their experiment.

Sources of Tension and Frustration

It was our conviction that these women were among the most highly frustrated of church personnel. The results of our study proved this to be so and underscored half a dozen factors as prime sources of that frustration.

The Environment: The abject misery and the inability to confront—much less change—the effects of hunger, disease, and unemployment, as well as the absence of beauty, were everywhere apparent.

A New Life-style: Conditions formerly taken for granted were no longer present. Personal health problems were caused by improper sanitation facilities, exhaustion, and poor diet, and there were cultural impoverishment and interpersonal problems.

Inadequacy of Structures: Overwork, exhaustion, and mental and physical breakdowns indicated the need for a set of structures functional to the new environment and responsive to its challenges. Having left behind the convential life-style and its formalities, which were protective of solitude and individual needs, these women were forced to create others that would allow for rest, recreation, and distance from the slum environment without reverting to alienating patterns.

Lack of Preparation: The difficulties encountered by a group of relatively well-educated women whose preparation had little or nothing to do with the exigencies of the environment were to be expected. Cultural privation and lack of stimulus were further aggravations.

Congregational Ties: Separated from other members of their congregations who were living in larger conventual institutions and were still devoted to teaching, these women in slum ministries often felt alienated, misunderstood, and abandoned. As a result ties with their larger congregations were often strained, adding to their sense of pain and frustration.

The Institutional Church: One of the prime sources of frustration was the church's attitude toward women in ministry. Almost 70 percent felt that the church's position with regard to the ordination of women was both illogical and inadmissible, while 80 percent resented the burden of responsibility without authority. Interestingly, the majority of the women interviewed for the 1976 study did not resent this at all, and the apparent contradiction offers further insight into the "women and ministry" issue. The differences between these two groups of women were substantial. The majority of those interviewed in 1976 were laywomen, not sisters. Their educational level was far lower and the extent of their dedication much more limited, ranging from two or three hours to a few days a week of pastoral service. The sisters living in slum areas were highly educated, completely dedicated to the ideal of service, identified by their very role with the institutional church, and therefore highly vulnerable with respect to its policies and deficiencies. To put it succinctly, they had more to lose. We point out again that the case of sisters is simply a more focused example of the position of all women in the Chilean church. When we wish to analyze a problem it is well to view it in its most advanced stage or, to put it differently, where the effects are most virulent.

Growth and Creativity in Spirituality

One of the principal hypotheses of the study stated that the experience of the women who were living and working in slum areas would make them more critical of the institutional church and less accepting of a literal interpretation of its teachings. Our findings showed that 66 percent of these women demonstrated a marked tendency to reinterpret doctrinal affirmations in search of a deeper significance rather than to hold to the absolutisms of total blind acceptance or total rejection. All of them attested to the fact that this position was a fairly new one in their lives. We were convinced that this was both an aspect and an indication of a larger dimension of their personal spirituality.

Results proved this to be true. Although plagued by incessant demands on their time, these women were not only more convinced than ever before in their lives of the necessity of personal and community prayer, revision of life in light of the gospel, and reflection days, but also and more important, they were more willing to make sacrifices to retain these as priorities.

Even in small houses, where space was extremely limited, 90 percent of the groups had set aside a small chapel or oratory, an eloquent testimony to the priority given to prayer.

The search for priestly direction, never an easy task in a society in which clerical numbers are waning, was a serious problem for 50 percent of these women. For more than 23 percent, however, a substitute had been discovered. They found excellent orientation in fellow religious and in their Christian communities, where sincerity and openness provided the best context for personal growth. This new form of spiritual direction deserved, we felt, some attention not only because it satisfied a need, but also because it constituted a form of spiritual and human growth that is at least as sound, if not sounder, than traditional forms of direction.

The results of this investigation show that the total ambience of these women had its effect not only as a source of frustration and tension, but also as a source of growth and creativity in their lives. The institutional church appeared, in many instances, to be cautious of them, of their growing self-awareness and the resulting conflictual relationship between institution and personnel.

Recapitulation

In a period spanning scarcely eleven years from the outset of our series of studies of women in the church, we can perceive the rather startling effects of changes initiated by Vatican II. The 1967 study disclosed large percentages of relatively well-educated women living in almost total alienation from their immediate surroundings. Many of them felt little or no obligation to serve the poor and less to conscienticize them; they saw little relation between the church's renewal and the need to reject wealth, power, and prestige. For them the highest priority was their own personal sanctification and, simple obedience to superiors, the best fulfillment of their commitment.

Our pulse taking in 1974 found women surprisingly active at all levels of ministry as the clerical crisis became endemic. Responsibility for the church's pastoral action was concretized particularly in the area of formation. Divergency between hierarchical and women's attitudes toward church and pastoral role models was emerging; views had evidently shifted and roles were undergoing a metamorphosis. This was particularly true among sisters included in the sample. It was clear that this group would provide a more focused case of what was happening among all women in the church. Their singleness of purpose, the dedication of their entire lives to the church's ministry made their secondary position —common to all women—that much more untenable and the need to face the issue unavoidable. For this reason the 1977 study centered on a particularly innovative group within their numbers, sisters living and working in slum areas.

It would be difficult to imagine a group more unlike our 1967 sample. The results portray a group whose attitudes and values stressed authenticity, liberation, solidarity, compassion, sensitivity, openness, sharing, confrontation, and respect for life. Their spirituality reflected definite interests, motives, and options, taking sides with the oppressed, the marginated, the poor in general; its basis lay in praxis, solidarity and shared experience. There was no dualism between sacred and profane, religious dimension and daily living. Their prayer and meditation reflected the reality of their life situation. Experience—the slum experience —had shaped their spirituality, altering values, attitudes, relations with the institutional church, vocational commitment, work, recreation, planning, prayer, and even their doctrinal stance. In the space of a decade a focused group of women within the church had come full circle.

The Way We Were

Change or reform never occurs evenly. On the contrary, it emerges in loosely associated rather than isolated pockets throughout the larger body, and it is this loose but real association that permits initial changes to mushroom and endure. Nonetheless, the question arises as to the possibility of reversal. The unanticipated consequences of Vatican II have thrown open the gates of ministry to women in the church. Obviously the result of the depletion of clerical ranks, the changes are nonetheless real, challenging and, to some, threatening. The question arises, if the numbers of vocations to the priesthood rise considerably in the near future, would it be possible to revert back to our former understanding of pastoral norms, structures, and roles?

The historical moment that has affected roles and pastoral images has also changed pastoral methods. Activities are now concentrated in the creation and vitalization of small communities. Their proliferation has required an ever-growing number of pastoral personnel, both men and women. The multiplication of such agents is therefore urgent; we will not need fewer personnel, but growing numbers to meet the demands of modern pastoral methods.

The Chilean hierarchy has not been static any more than has history. If we were to question the bishops today with respect to their views on women in ministry, the results would doubtless be different. The Third General Conference of Latin-American Bishops was held in Puebla, Mexico, in early 1979, and its pastoral implications have made radical change the only possible response of a pilgrim church. Change initiated by Vatican II and confirmed by Medellín now adopted the particular contours determined by a strong "option for the poor." Pastoral priorities, methods, and means have all undergone transformations determined by that same option, and bishops, pastoral personnel, and laity have been deeply affected in the process. Nothing can ever be the same, and that is likewise true for the image of women in the church. Having become incorporated into responsible pastoral action, women have been unconsciously engaged in changing that image. The prevailing feminine image in any historical period is only a reflection of the dominant value system. If the image has begun to crack, we can be sure that cultural values are subject to the same process; once initiated, the process makes any thought of reversal an illusion. Putting the "toothpaste back in the tube"[9] will be an ever more unthinkable option. However, more important than any sense of accomplishment is the certainty that such changes are not transient and have in fact been absorbed and transmitted by the almost imperceptible forces of socialization. It is with this in mind that the results of our fourth and last study are presented.

New Wine in New Wineskins

Having focused in on a particularly vulnerable group of women in the church in earlier studies, we continued in this vein, hoping to gain further insights into changes already initiated among women religious. In 1982, at the urging of the hierarchy and of those directly involved in the formation of women religious, a study was begun among young candidates to religious life in Chilean novitiates throughout the country.[10] We include here only those elements pertinent to our analysis. Of the 238 young women interviewed, 83 percent had not yet been born or were just taking their first tottering steps as Vatican II convened in 1962. Having grown up in a church that was radically different from that of their parents, it was our assumption that the wine of their religious commitment would need, and hopefully encounter, "new wineskins." The results of our investigation proved our assumption to be at least partially valid and offered startling contrasts with the 1967 study.

The responses of these young women showed that almost 60 percent of the congregations they represented were serving the poorest sectors of society in a variety of ministries. Although education remained the ministry with the highest percentage of involvement, it had dropped from a 75 percent majority in 1967 to only 51 percent in 1982; from a service to the middle and upper classes, it had shifted to an emphasis on the children of laborers and other urban poor.

The lack of personal liberty in the lives of women religious was painfully evident in the 1967 responses. The sisters, in great part, were not permitted normal friendships and a social life with laypeople, or even to visit their students. The majority wore habits, were assigned to their ministries by superiors, and were dependent on them for every need. Now many young candidates, even during the usually cloistered years of novitiate formation, were visiting homes and were involved in youth groups and classes with adults. In 47 percent of the congregations represented, the use of secular clothing was permitted on many occasions, and in 11 percent, no type of uniform clothing was worn. In 42 percent of these congregations, members selected their ministries in accord with personal talents, after dialogue with superiors, and in another 38 percent, selection was made only after long mutual deliberation. Thirty-three percent of these congregations give members a stated amount of money regularly to cover personal expenses. Major superiors still name local superiors in 77 percent of cases, but in the remainder they either are elected by members of the local house or are simply coordinators rather than superiors, or else there is no one with special authority in the group.

In the 1960s religious congregations in Chile requested that candidates to religious life bring letters of recommendation from pastors along with proofs of a blameless life; now a high school diploma, previous pastoral experience, and a discernment process are required. The motivation behind the decision of these women to enter the novitiate is no longer specifically "the love of God" or a sense of "calling," as it was in 1967, but instead the specific work of the congregation of their choice (31%) and the opportunity to carry out a concrete option for the poor (30%). When we consider that this last was the least mentioned motivation for entering in the 1967 study (2%), the change becomes more evident. A subtle modification can be noted in the shift to service (80%) from a spirituality emphasizing prayer, silence, and spiritual perfection (14%).

Perhaps the greatest contribution to the implementation of Vatican II was a program for novitiate formation, initiated in the late 1960s and offered by the Confederation of the Religious of Chile (CONFERRE). As part of an extensive renewal program, all congregations of active religious were invited to send their young candidates to formal classes in biblical, theological, and psychological formation. Almost 60 percent of our sample attended these weekly classes, and their congregations were clearly distinguishable for their strong preferential option for the poor and for the relatively high level of personal liberty permitted by their structures. It is evident that the rich interchange between congregations permitted by CONFERRE has deepened the identification of candidates and their congregations with the pastoral plans of their hierarchy and the spirit of renewal.

Summing Up

The writing of a chapter such as this can be most illuminating even for the author. The intricate interweaving of historical events, innovative action, and empirical data and the patina of time can offer insights into the rather startling amount of change that has transpired. Caught in the day-to-day struggle, one is perhaps more aware of conflict and its effects. The sociological significance of conflict has never been disputed, but we would be hard put to declare it welcome. Welcome or not, woman's coming of age in the church has been and will continue to prove conflictual. This is not a problem, but a process, not anyone's victory, but a series of interlocking conflicts designed to resolve divergent dualisms, and the process itself is functional to the end pursued. Whatever the outcome within our lifetime, we shall never be quite the same again.

We could easily be made to believe that nothing has happened and yet we have changed as a house changes into which a guest has entered. . . . The future enters into us in this way to transform itself in us long before it happens.[11]

5

Catholic Women of India

Stella Faria

Before the Second Vatican Council the Catholic Church, patterned after the Council of Trent, was pyramidical in structure and authoritarian in practice. The pope was at the top, followed by cardinals, bishops, priests, and religious, with laity at the base. The women and men who composed the laity assumed that in order to be a good "practicing" Catholic it was sufficient to "pray, pay, obey" and sacramentalize; they did not participate in the decision-making bodies or in the mission of the church. Vatican II, in its vision that every member share in the total life of the church, brought about the possibility of change by opening up new ways for laywomen and laymen to contribute to the development and mission of the church. Vatican II documents affirmed this new direction:

> Since in our times women have an ever more active share in the whole life of society, it is very important that they participate more widely also in the various fields of the Church's apostolate.[1]

The changes brought about by Vatican II enabled women to participate in all lay ministries of the church. These include such ministries as labor, mass communication, youth, the poor and downtrodden, education, the welfare of women, evangelization, and music. The priesthood remains closed to women, and Pope John Paul II has forbidden further discussion of that subject. However, Canon 230-3 states:

> Where the needs of the Church require and ministers are not available, lay people, even though they are not lectors or acolytes, can supply certain of their functions, that is, exercise the ministry of the word, preside over liturgical prayers, confer baptism and distribute Holy Communion, in accordance with the provisions of the law.

This statement was confirmed by Archbishop Angelo Fernandes of Delhi when he said, "Both men and women could undertake liturgical and sacramental functions, such as conferring Baptism, and distributing Communion and to preach the Word of God in Churches, on occasions specified by the Episcopal Conferences."[2]

What has this redefinition of the role of the laity in general and of women in particular meant for Catholic women in India? Both as laity and as women they have occupied the bottom rung in the church hierarchy. In addition, as Indians, they are part of a society that both traditionally and even now, despite provisions in the constitution to the contrary, considers women to be inferior to men. For example, the 1981 census showed only 935 females for every 1,000 males in the population, even though their numbers were equal at birth; female literacy is only 24.88 percent as against 46.74 percent for men. In assessing the situation of Catholic women within the church in India today, this chapter provides first a general overview of the place of laywomen in church structures and then a more detailed description of women religious as well as of the Council of Catholic Women of India.

Opportunities for laywomen being involved in a wide range of activities are available in theory. What is happening in practice? At the parish level many Catholic women are readers, spiritual animators, and guides, and teach catechesis. Except in movements like Marriage Encounter, Christian Family Movement, and the Charismatic Renewal, in which married couples participate together, women are more actively engaged than men in works of healing, charity, family welfare and family life education, natural family planning, and counseling. Women are also elected members of parish and pastoral councils. At the national level, women and men, religious and lay, may be nominated by the Catholic Bishops' Conference of India (CBCI)[3] to serve as consultors to the five CBCI commissions: Christian Life, Proclamation, Justice and Development, Clergy and Religious, and Laity. Consultors are nominated on the basis of their expertise on subjects under consideration and their involvement in church activities. They do not serve for a specific term but are invited to those meetings at which their opinion and expertise can make a useful contribution. In addition, women are on the National Advisory Council (NAC) to the CBCI. The NAC is a consultative body of eighty-five members representing all sections of the Catholic Church in India —bishops, priests, religious, and laity. On the international level, women are appointed to a few pontifical commissions that meet in Rome. The members of these commissions are appointed by the pope. They serve five-year terms and represent Catholics in different parts of the world.

In recent years the Laity Commission of the CBCI has given special attention to women. It accepted the request of its four women consultors, made in August 1982, to hold a National Consultation of Women. This took place in June 1984. In December 1983 the Laity Commission held a Lay Leaders Convention at which 230 female and male participants debated crucial issues concerning the role of the laity in the leadership of the church. The following statement of the Convention indicates their desire for a wider role for women in the church.

> Women, both Lay and Religious, have made a tremendous contribution to the authentic growth of the Church. However, in practice, their role and status have not been fully recognized in the Church. They have not been given the representation they deserve in ecclesial bodies, such as Parish and Pastoral Councils.[4]

They recommended that

> the role and status of women be fully recognised and given adequate representation in the Pastoral Councils and other ecclesial bodies. Their professional participation in theologising should be fostered, and all discrimination on the basis of sex for lay ministries in the Church, in accordance with the New Code of Canon Lay, should be removed. The Church should also take active part in fighting the discrimination that is present against women within the law of the country.[5]

Although their emphasis is on theological formation instead of increased representation in ecclesial bodies, the hierarchy appear to agree that attention must be given to the needs of the laity in the life of the church. Pope John Paul II, in his message to the Asian meeting of the Pontifical Council for the Laity held in Hong Kong, said, "My conviction is that the spiritual, moral and theological formation of lay men and *women* is one of the most urgent priorities in the Church, if we are fully to put the teaching of Vatican II into effect."[6] Awakening to the urgent need in India, the meeting of the CBCI in Nagpur in January and February of 1984 echoed this same view in stating that "high pastoral priority has to be given to the formation of lay men and women" who "should be provided opportunities for a spiritual theological formation with special emphasis on the social doctrine of the Church."[7] At this writing these recommendations of the CBCI and of its Laity Commission are no more than statements of good intentions. Whether, when, and how they will be implemented remains to be seen.

Women Religious in India

The Catholic Church in India has 166 religious congregations of women actively involved in apostolic works. Of these, 102 are of foreign origin[8] and sixty-four are indigenous, the first having been founded in

Kerala, South India, in 1831. In 1960 the women religious federated under the auspices of the Conference of Religious in India (CRI). The aims of the CRI are to (a) share the experience of their religious commitment; (b) be helped as a group in the fulfillment of their prophetic function, and (c) promote joint endeavor in the church's apostolate. There are three times as many sisters as priests and brothers combined. The number of women religious personnel in comparison with men is shown in Table II.[9] Women religious have increased from 16,369 in 1959 to approximately 50,000 in 1984. The overwhelming majority of sisters (77% in 1981) come from the state of Kerala.[10]

Table II. Religious Personnel of the Catholic Church in India by Category, 1981		
Category	*Number*	*Percentage*
Nuns	45,462	75.4
Priests	12,386	20.6
Brothers	2,411	4.0
Total	60,259	100.0

Women religious in India have made a remarkable contribution to the church and to the country in terms of education, health services, and community development. More than half the sisters are engaged in educational institutions from the primary school to the university level. They have distinguished themselves through their emphasis on character formation, personality development, and moral education. In South India, for instance, the Apostolic Carmel Sisters in Mangalore began the first Catholic college for women, St. Agnes College, in 1923. Most of the primary and high schools run by congregations were founded for girls only.

In the field of health the sisters' efficiency and dedication is visible in both sophisticated nursing homes and simple rural clinics. Much importance is given to rural and community health programs, with special attention to the curative, preventive, and social aspects of medicine. The Catholic Hospital Association of India (CHAI) was founded through the vision and initiative of an Australian woman doctor, Sister Mary Glowrey, in July 1943. Today CHAI has 1,620 members in different parts of the country.[11] The chief aims of CHAI are to improve the standards of hospitals and dispensaries; to promote, realize, and safeguard progressively higher ideals in all phases of health welfare programs; and to assist voluntary health organizations to procure quality amenities, equipment, and medicines at low cost.

In the field of community development, women religious try to liberate the poor and oppressed from the bonds of backwardness, inhuman conditions, and health hazards caused by ignorance, poverty, and malnutrition. The sisters work through education, health services, nutritional programs, hostels for working women, orphanages, and crèches in their attempt to improve the socioeconomic condition of these people.

Table III shows the growth of Catholic institutions in India from 1948 to 1976.[12] Most of these institutions are run by sisters. Despite their tremendous contribution to and participation in the growth of Catholic institutions, as well as in the total life and mission of the church, women religious have been held back by many factors in their own personal growth and development. On the one hand they are afforded opportunities for specialization in various fields of activity (e.g., medicine, nursing, administration, community development); on the other hand they are bound by congregational structures.

After Vatican II the rigid structures of the female congregations were replaced by more adaptable ones that lay greater emphasis on achieving harmony with the "present day physical and psychological condition of the members."[13] The old order had been challenged and new freedoms given. However, the new liberative philosophy has not meant total liberation for all women religious, many of whom remain oppressed within their own constitutional framework. To change or break traditional practices and structures that have fossilized over a long period is difficult. There is an awareness of the problems of outmoded structures, so change is inevitable in the future. Other factors that retard the sisters' growth are a poor self-image, life-style, and cultural alienation.

Many women religious have a poor image of themselves as women.[14] They are identified by their religious vocation and work and not by who they are as individuals. The structures and tradition have made them dependent on priests for every act they perform, be it the writing of their congregation's constitution or spiritual guidance. Their dependence has made them appear intellectually inferior to men and, consequently, only a few sisters are included in ecclesial, decision-making, and administrative bodies. The few usually include those who are in charge of educational institutions, hospitals, and community development projects as well as generals, superiors, and the president of the CRI. Even though some sisters have received theological training, hardly any of them are teaching in theological seminaries. Generally, "sisters are treated as cogwheels in a big machine with disregard to their own personality."[15] In the church, women religious belong to the category of, and are treated as, laywomen despite their highly respected celibate status, which in

Table III. Growth of Catholic Institutions in India, 1948–1976

Year	Primary Schools	High Schools	Colleges and Universities	Hospitals	Dispensaries	Homes for Aged	Leprosaria	Homes for Destitute
1948	4,096	1,526	30	53	157	58	11	17
1958	N.A.	N.A.	N.A.	119	474	75	10	20
1968	4,877	2,196	78	228	629	76	36	19
1976	5,176	3,886	130	508	1,068	136	85[a]	47[b]

a. The sudden rise is accounted for by a group in Jamshedpur that has started a massive Leprosy Prevention Program.

b. The new houses are mainly those of Mother Teresa's Missionaries of Charity.

India is considered to be one of the highest virtues. These factors, plus being left out of the organizational work of the church, have contributed to the sisters' poor self-image.

As a result of the Western congregations in India, many Indian sisters are expected to adapt to a Western way of life. They find it difficult to change to life-styles, eating habits, languages, and modes of dress that may be unfamiliar to them. Adapting to a Western, usually meaning a more affluent, higher-class, life-style not only makes them feel different from other Indian women, but it is also an impediment to their identification with the poor, whom the church and religious congregations are seeking to serve. They are caught between being geared to the "cause of the weak and downtrodden"[16] and being expected to adopt a Western life-style. Only a few of the indigenous congregations and individual sisters have tried to adapt their life-style to that of the poor and become truly integrated with the people they serve. Mother Teresa and her Missionaries of Charity are notable examples.

Closely associated with life-style is the problem of cultural alienation. In foreign congregations Western music, art, literature, and values are encouraged to the detriment of Indian culture. Because sisters are cut off from their own heritage, Indian culture and cultural values do not receive the importance they deserve. In turn the poor internalize the Western cultural values they learn from and observe in the sisters who work with them.

The same problem of institutionalization or restrictive structures that hinders women religious in their own personal growth and development also hinders them from improving the lot of their poverty-stricken sisters outside the convent walls. One concerned sister has said, "We are not free like lay women to just take up a case and fight for it. On the other hand we have the advantage as a group of already being well organised. But, like an army, unless our officers give the word, we may not march."[17] This same sister is of the firm opinion that superiors are too busy with administrative tasks to give priority to the problems besetting the world outside their own. While they hesitate to "take the risk of urging us to emerge from our institution and pitch in with others, precious time is being lost and so much personnel and energy, so many resources are being blocked. What a colossal waste!"[18] This may be true, but it must also be said that serious attempts at an examination of their own value system have been made. CRI discussions and meetings have focused on such themes as "The Aspirations of a Just Society and the Role of Women Religious" (1973) and "Difficulties in Rural Apostolate" (1979) in an effort by women religious to understand and live their vocation.

More and more young sisters, awakening to the reality of the suffering and dehumanization of more than 65 percent of the population, are striving to break away from the bonds of institutionalization and are voicing their resentment at the unhealthy structures. When all 50,000 sisters join hands with one another on this matter they will create a force to be reckoned with! The national CRI has realized the need to be a catalyst for a change and has committed itself to *work with* the poor in order to organize them and help them to live lives that are more human, to train *youth* for leadership, decision making, and political and national involvement, and, finally, to work with *the masses of women* in order to liberate them from apathy, fatalism, and age-old traditions and customs. This commitment is for the sake of the church in India, which is poor, which is the church of the young, and at the same time a church that is awakening.[19]

The Council of Catholic Women of India

The Council of Catholic Women of India (CCWI) was founded as a direct result of the Eucharistic Congress held in Bombay in December 1964. It was at this Congress that Catholic women in India and the late Countess Christine de Hamptine of Belgium, then a board member of the World Union of Catholic Women's Organizations, gathered together to exchange views on organizing Indian women at a national level. In their dialogue these women discovered themselves and saw what a power they could be for the church and the nation if they were organized. On December 7, 1964, an ad hoc committee was formed to study both the position of women's organizations in the different dioceses and the possibility of coordinating them at a national level. In September 1966, after being officially sanctioned by Archbishop Eugene D'Souza, chairman of the Lay Apostolate section of the CBCI, the National Council of Catholic Women of India was inaugurated in Nagpur.

The aims of the CCWI are to coordinate the activities of Catholic women in the civic, social, cultural, educational, economic, and religious fields. It strives to serve as a medium by which women can speak on matters of public and personal interest. In addition, it aims to develop the social consciousness of women by creating an awareness of their duty to the weaker sections of society.

The CCWI is a federation of affiliated, autonomous units at the parish, diocesan, and regional levels. Parish units are called Catholic women's leagues or fellowships. Several leagues form a Diocesan Council of Catholic Women (DCCW). DCCWs are grouped under ecclesiastical regions formed on the basis of linguistic divisions. The National Secretariat in Bangalore coordinates the activities of the seventy-eight diocesan units composed of approximately 100,000 women.[20] An Executive Committee of ten or twelve members, including a president, vice-president, general secretary, and treasurer, meets semiannually to review the CCWI's role, functions, programs, and activities; to decide policy matters; and to plan national meetings and conferences.

The general body of the CCWI meets triennially at a national conference. Each diocese sends two voting delegates and pays their expenses. Other women can go at their own expense without voting rights. Every three years the delegates use this occasion to elect members to the Executive Committee. The themes of the conferences are chosen for their relevance to Catholic women and to current situations. (See Table IV.) The themes are discussed and debated, and resolutions are passed. For example, at these conferences the council has resolved to ensure that every Catholic woman is on the electoral rolls; to eradicate illiteracy, especially among women; and to right the wrongs done to women. This will be done by starting counseling cells and disseminating information about women's rights. Highlights of the conferences and proposals to implement the resolutions passed at the executive meetings are published in *Neythri* (The Woman Leader), the official monthly bulletin of the CCWI.

Projects were initiated in parts of India during 1968–69 so that the predominantly urban-based units of the CCWI could reach out to rural women. In addition, the projects were to enable diocesan groups to develop leadership among their members and at the same time make them aware of their social responsibility. The CCWI received assistance from Catholic women in Germany, Holland, Belgium, and Switzerland to begin more than twenty of these projects. (See Table V.) Although this work added a new dimension to the CCWI[21] and indicated a serious attempt to reach women at the grass roots, its result is difficult to assess, for no follow-up evaluations or reports were made.

Development activities for education, health, and social welfare have been taken up by the units. Much has been done in the field of education, with the units providing scholarships and free uniforms for children as well as running adult literacy classes. Health service programs have included immunization, natural family planning, milk and nutrition schemes for rural children, hospital visits, and work in leper asylums. Economic activities range from fancy fetes, fund raising, and jumble sales to collecting advertisements and donations. Christmas functions, picnics, and dance dramas have been organized to aid poor children. Leadership camps for personality development, particularly in the Northeast, where 1,500 to 2,000 women participate, have been conducted regularly by local units. Spiritual activities include ecumenical prayer meetings, such as the World Day of Prayer and Christian Unity Week, occasional Bible study classes, and short theology courses.

Table IV. National Conferences of the CCWI

Year	Place	Theme	Number Attended
1966	Nagpur	Organization of the Catholic Women of India on a National Basis	100
1967	Madras	The Dual Role of the India Catholic Woman in the Family and the Nation	200
1968	Ernakulam	The Indian Catholic Woman— A Power for Integration	500
1969	Bhopal	The Indian Catholic Woman in Civic and Public Life	100
1970	Ranchi	The Indian Catholic Woman— Her Christian Responsibilities	350 approx.
1971	Goa	Women in Dialogue	150
1972	Delhi	Social and Moral Rehabilitation of Women	100
1973	Bangalore	Women and Liberation	228
1974	Bombay	Population—Our Concern	181
1975	Calcutta	Integral Woman: Equality, Development, and Peace	250
1978[a]	Ajmer	The Role of the Catholic Woman in the Ongoing Process of Social, Economic, and Cultural Change in India Today	200
1981	Vijayawada	Woman and the Eucharist	300

a. The national conferences were held annually until 1975 and thereafter triennially.

Table V. Projects Financed by the CCWI: 1969–1978

Diocese	Project	Year
Madurai	Educational project	1969
Tiruchirapalli	Welfare project, craft training (tailoring)	1969
Cochin	Project for a weaving center	1969
Changancherry	Craft training (sewing), farm project (poultry)	1969
Dharwar	Poultry project	1969
Trivandrum (Syrian)	Needlework and garment making, medical care, poultry project	1969
Madras	Kilacheri project, rural service project	1969
Vellore	Welfare project	1970
Ootacamund	Craft training (sewing)	1972
Trivandrum (Latin)	Cottage industry	1973
Bellary	Project of hygienic education of the citizens	1973
Nagercoil	Welfare project (providing work for young unemployed girls)	1974
Alleppey	Cottage industry	1974
Bombay	Project of the low-income hostel and polytechnic, Development of the women of Uplat village	1974
Honnavar	Women's welfare project (Balwadi)[a]	1974
Ullal	Ullal community development project	1974
Bangalore	Silverpura project (Nirmala health center)	1974
Shevgaon	Craft training (kitchen gardening), Balwadis	1974
Pavoor	Beedi rolling project	1975
Calcutta	Multipurpose project for women's education	1975
Ranchi	Catholic Mahila Sangh[b]	1975
Patna	Carmel Technical Institute	1976
Mangalore	Shubada project (rehabilitation center)	1978

a. Nursery school
b. Women's association

Neythri has published several good articles on the role and status of women, natural family planning, population, psychology, and social change. Reports of the diocesan and regional units have been regular features. Sometimes recipes, which most Indian women's magazines carry a surfeit of, are printed. This space could be much better used to publish information related to women's laws, rights, and obligations as well as statistics on women's literacy, population, and employment. This kind of information would be educative and stimulating for the reader. *Neythri* should be, as its name suggests, a "Woman Leader."

In reviewing the work of the CCWI over the past twenty years, its major achievements have been receiving official recognition and status as a national body by the CBCI; building a network with other women's organizations and ecumenical groups, both in India and abroad; giving women from different parts of the country an opportunity to come together to share their experiences; and establishing a secretariat with a full-time secretary in Bangalore in 1972.

In an attempt to evaluate the council's work, a questionnaire was sent in February 1984 to a sample of twenty drawn from the Executive Committee, founding members, and leaders from different parts of the country. Replies regarding the CCWI's goals and performance differed. The following quotes show the diverse opinion: "In some ways goals are fulfilled"; "Too broad, which has resulted in the achievements being slow and painful"; "Solidarity among women has yet to be achieved"; "Outside factors are forever militating against any kind of union and understanding between members of half of humanity"; "Cooperation of the hierarchy is not forthcoming." Others believed that matters of vital importance need attention and pointed out that several long-time members had resigned because of various factors.

My own assessment is that the council's growth has been stifled chiefly because two or three persons have, from its inception, guided its destiny and spelled out its policy and programs. For this reason some women who, in responding to the questionnaire, wished to become more involved in CCWI affairs also expressed their fear of being ineffective. The situation can be rectified only by the induction of new blood into the administration of the CCWI.

As the CCWI looks toward the future, several things should be done to help it fulfill its aims and live up to its motto: "in the service of Church and nation." An organizing secretary should be hired who can visit and revive units, formulate programs, encourage women to become involved, sensitize women about their role, and help them to discern and to prioritize. The council should tap the potential of women, gear them to action, and make sure every unit makes a commitment that is worthy of its membership. Members should stop depending on the hierarchy and look instead to themselves in planning and promoting their own cause.

Some new things are already occurring that indicate the CCWI's potential, influence, and power for the future. In 1982 the Executive Committee members indulged in a bit of introspection and concluded that theirs was an elitist organization that catered mainly to upper- and middle-class Catholic women. Realizing that, despite special projects, they had not really touched the grass roots, a few members requested the CBCI Laity Commission to organize a National Consultation of Women in order to make them aware of their role in the church and society and to educate them about their rights and obligations. The Laity Commission took this request seriously. It formed a core team to plan a national consultation, which was held in Bombay in June 1984. This team was made up of the chairman and secretary of the Laity Commission, a few CCWI members, and some other women. Invited to the consultation were members of the core team, member bishops of the Laity Commission, the Indian representative of the Pontifical Commission for the Laity, and about one hundred others, mostly women, including members of the CCWI and CRI. The consultation was important not only because women received the cooperation of the church's hierarchy in organizing it but also because it was an opportunity to awaken women to play their role in the church and society and to be prophetic instruments of justice, peace, and love.

In preparation for the National Consultation and as a way to focus attention on women, the CBCI declared February 12, 1984, as Women's Sunday. A special liturgy was prepared by the National Biblical, Catechetical, and Liturgical Centre for this landmark occasion, which was celebrated in all the dioceses in India. This was the first time that the Catholic Church in India had honored women by dedicating a special day to them. To give content to the consultation, three women edited a special volume entitled *The Emerging Christian Woman: Church and Society Perspectives.* [22] In addition, as part of the preparatory process, meetings were organized at the parish, diocesan, and regional levels.

Conclusions

The Catholic Church in India, in attempting to move forward in the directions set by Vatican II, has had to overcome the inertia created by both its own churchly traditions and Indian sociocultural traditions with regard to women. Neither the 50,000 sisters belonging to the CRI nor the 100,000 members of the CCWI can be considered typical of the some 5 million Catholic women in India today. Yet, as potential catalysts of change, they do provide some insights into the new possibilities now open to the Catholic women of India, as well as into some of the obstacles still to be overcome if the vision of Vatican II is to be realized.

Despite unjust structures and socioeconomic disparities, religious and laywomen have played a very active role. The church needs the full participation of both women and men. Women have recognized the signs of the times. Imbued with the Spirit, they are determined to win not the battle of the sexes but a place in the universal order where women and men are truly compatible and can together make real the mission of the Redeemer.

6

Cultural Ambivalence
and Ceremonial Leadership:
The Role of Women in Africa's
New Religions

Bennetta Jules-Rosette

M ore than seven thousand new religious movements exist in sub-Saharan Africa today. Together, they claim more than 32 million adherents.[1] Many of these movements have arisen in areas in which there has been intensive contact with Christian missionary efforts. However, prophetic and messianic movements in Africa predate European contact. These early movements may be considered to have established the cultural background for more recent developments, and as early as the eighteenth century, women appeared as leaders of the prophetic sects and cults. The new groups differ from one another in terms of their history, organizational structure, and doctrinal base. Although the term "new religions" has been used in the United States to refer to religious and consciousness movements arising in the 1960s and continuing through the present, in the African context such groups may be traced to the 1920s and have much deeper historical roots in precolonial religious and protest movements.

There are three major types of new religious movements: (1) indigenous or independent churches that arose outside mission control; (2) separatist churches that have broken away from missions; and (3) neotraditional cults. Only the first two types will be considered here. Specifically, I shall analyze three indigenous churches established by women and one separatist group. Both the indigenous and the separatist groups have manifested themselves in different social and historical forms in central, southern, and East Africa. They blend elements of traditional religions with the influence of historic and modern churches.[2] The roles played by women and their limited access to leadership positions follow similar patterns in the independent churches and in the separatist movements.

There are few serious studies of the role of women in new African religions and they are relatively recent. Moreover, as the rank and file members of such movements, women possess their own hidden subcultures and practices that are not readily accessible to outsiders. Research on women and religion arising from a feminist perspective has tended to exclude the new African groups and to turn away from the cross-cultural subtleties in gender relations and cultural practices that these groups contain. Separation of men and women in seating arrangements, ritual activities, and social events is common in both mission and new churches in Africa. This separation may, in many cases, be traced to accepted cultural practices of separation, secrecy, and seclusion in traditional men's and women's activities. But rather than focusing on these practices, this study examines some key themes that surround women's participation in new African religions in an effort to understand the unique positions that women hold as symbolic and cultural leaders.

Although there have been notable exceptions, women have, for the most part, *not* been the founders and principal leaders of Africa's new religious movements. They have, however, played decisive symbolic and organizational roles. It is essential to differentiate between those religious organizations in which women exercise some degree of political leadership and those that promote the ceremonial influence of women. Ceremonial leadership offers women the possibility to rise to positions of privilege in Africa's new churches without holding positions of political authority.[3] It relies heavily on cultural and gender-linked stereotypes. Such leadership is generally limited to specific ritual and social contexts. Ceremonial leadership is essentially symbolic and does not imply the direct exercise of power and legitimate authority within a group. Consequently, women who exercise ceremonial leadership may be wise or respected charismatic figures, whose actual role in the governance of religious organizations is indirect or highly circumscribed.

If my observations concerning the role of women in Africa's new religious organizations are correct, one may ask why they join. Four basic wishes expressed by women who are adherents of Africa's new religious movements provide a key for analyzing ritual and doctrine in a variety of religious movements and for fathoming the collective and individual motivations of women who join these groups.

    1. The wish to change the social order by means of instituting a new religious order
    2. The wish to alter conventionally accepted relationships between males and females in a given cultural and historical context
    3. The wish to alleviate the physical, moral, and emotional suffering of women through the new religious order
    4. The wish to enact these changes and the belief that these wishes will be fulfilled through ceremonies and daily religious practice

The new African religious movements attempt to change social reality through symbolic means. Women are motivated to join such movements to alter their own life conditions, on the symbolic level if not in actual terms. This process may be seen in perspective with reference to the history of such movements in several African contexts.

Historical Overview of Women in African Cults and Churches

Among the earliest women leaders in the eighteenth-century groups preceding the new religions were Fumaria, reportedly a charismatic seer, and Dona Béatrice-Anthony, a visionary who claimed to be the reincarnation of Anthony of Padua.[4] Little is known about Fumaria apart from her claim to have visions and direct revelations from the Virgin Mary through which she reportedly received the power to detect and punish sins. Béatrice appeared in the Kongo Kingdom of San Salvador during the early 1700s. Her following grew large enough to be labeled a heretical break from the Catholic Church. The prophetess challenged the Portuguese Capuchin missionaries, urging her followers to return to polygyny and traditional family units, abandon the symbols of the Catholic Church, purify themselves with rain water, and oust priests from the kingdom.[5] Béatrice assured her followers of the messianic coming of princes who would restore the line of Kongo kingship. An African "Joan of Arc," she was burned at the stake by the Catholic Church and gained immortality in the legends that survived her.

There is little clear documentation from the nineteenth century concerning the role of women in African religious movements. However, the life of one exceptional woman, Madam Yoko, Paramount Chief of the Kpa Mende kingdom of Sierra Leone from 1884 to 1896, has been well documented. Although not strictly a religious cult leader, Madam Yoko based her power, in part, on her position in the Sande women's secret society that shares leadership responsibilities with the counterpart male secret society, the Poro. Madam Yoko succeeded her husband in office but was able to extend her influence and control far beyond the area that he governed. Thirteen years after her death, her kingdom was destroyed by factionalism and warfare.[6]

It was not, however, until the turn of the century that a number of popular movements began to appear in which women played significant roles as ceremonial and prophetic figures. The Déima cult was an offshoot of the prophetic movement founded by the Liberian prophet William Wade Harris in 1913.[7] Established in 1940 by Marie Dahonon Lalou, a Godié woman from the Ivory Coast, the Déima movement emphasized healing through the use of a special form of holy water said to have been obtained from serpents. Following the example of some of the traditional mediums and diviners in her area, Marie Lalou renounced marriage and sexual contact. She virtually became a "ritual man," no longer subject to the traditional roles of other Godié women. In so doing she fulfilled the second wish: the transformation of relationships between men and women through ritual. Four aspects of the Déima cult are crucial to the discussion of women's status: (1) that Lalou, its founder, was a woman; (2) that some of the activities of women were conceived of as being ritually exclusive to them even though male adepthood was involved; (3) that ceremonial leadership required celibacy; and (4) that healing, often related to the women's nurturing role, was one of the cult's major concerns. Several leaders made abortive attempts to succeed Marie Lalou. One was a woman who was unable to maintain group support for her leadership.

The tradition of spirit mediumship became a resource for women who were founders of new religious groups. A handful can be named: Mai ("Mother") Chaza in Zimbabwe, Alice Lenshina Mulenga in Zambia, Marie Lalou in the Ivory Coast, and Gaudencia Aoko in Kenya. Mai Chaza was an extraordinarily charismatic figure whose claims to spiritual power largely paralleled those of male leaders in the Shona churches. She was a former Methodist who was inspired by spiritual revelations to begin her healing ministry. In 1954, Mai Chaza allegedly "died" and was resurrected. According to her account, during her death she had communicated with God and had been given the spiritual gift of healing. She received further spiritual inspiration on a mountain, afterward dubbed Sinai, and was commanded to abstain from alcohol, all sexual activities, and traditional medicines.

Mai Chaza regarded sexual abstinence as increasing her spiritual potency. From a symbolic and social perspective, sexual abstinence removes leaders such as Mai Chaza from the conventional roles of wife and mother. They assume the status of "ritual males"—a role that is common among the traditional female healer-diviners. Through renouncing the status of an "ordinary woman," these women have achieved spiritual and ceremonial leadership but have been unable to pass their positions on to another woman.[8] Moreover, these women have rejected conventional social and cultural roles primarily for spiritual purposes and not as a source of social equality. Consequently, a cultural ambivalence arises between their religious status as spiritual leaders and their secular social positions as women.

Mai Chaza returned with the mission to heal women who were barren, those who were possessed by alien spirits, and the blind. Her success drew large numbers of followers, estimated at 70,000 by the late 1950s. She established holy villages, called Cities of God (Guta ra Jehovah), in which she cared for the sick—first at Seke, then at Zumunya, Zuimba,

Harare, and Bulawayo in Zimbabwe. At these healing centers, members were urged to confess publicly and were then cared for through special healing ceremonies and exorcisms.

To establish her unique position, Mai Chaza built on the prominence of the ritual woman in Shona tradition. By using the methods of a spirit medium and traditional doctor, she achieved a position of power through forms of self-expression already legitimately available to women. The woman with such charismatic powers is perceived as equal to male religious leaders. Mai Chaza, however, made no provision for female succession in her movement, and her own daughters did not follow her in leadership positions.

Shortly after her death, in 1960, Mai Chaza was succeeded by a male Malawian, Mapaulos, who began to perform extraordinary healings in her name. He assumed the title *Vamutenga* ("he who is sent from heaven") and continued his mission at Mai Chaza's healing centers. Mapaulos, who usually appeared in public under a veil, claimed not only to have prophetic and healing powers, but also to be an incarnation-of God. Such claims were perhaps useful when he assumed the status of Mai Chaza, who was viewed as a black messiah, equated by her followers with both Moses and Jesus.[9]

In the same year that Mai Chaza received her spiritual calling, Alice Lenshina Mulenga reportedly "died" and came back to life with a religious mission. Naming her new church *Lumpa,* the "highest" or the "supreme" in the Bemba language, Lenshina promised her followers health and a new life if they abandoned traditional magic and witchcraft to follow her. She established a holy village at Kasomo, in northern Zambia, and proclaimed the political and religious autonomy of her followers in the "New Zion." Reputed to have become aligned with the African National Congress, a former Zambian political party, Lenshina's followers refused to pay their taxes, and in 1964 they defended their village with armed and violent opposition to the newly independent Zambian government. These activities eventually led to the expulsion of Lenshina's followers from Zambia in 1970. The cohesiveness of the Lumpa movement was destroyed through political struggles. Although Lenshina's group began as a prophetic, anticolonialist movement, it failed to integrate itself into the new nation-state as a legitimate and accepted religious organization. Lenshina was also unable to name a female successor to lead her church after her death, in the late 1970s.[10]

Although similar in conception, Lenshina's and Mai Chaza's holy communities relied on different idioms and concepts of leadership. However, Lenshina could draw on the precedent of institutionalized power and authority granted to women as leaders among the matrilineal Bemba. Although her activities in healing and antisorcery added a new element, Lenshina's regulation of the community and the apparent secular ties indicate that the Lumpa Church offered its members significant means of access to power in the larger political arena. It would seem likely that women who are not priestesses or preachers would concentrate on supportive positions at a lower level by participating through ceremony. However, ceremonial influence, as exemplified by Lenshina's case, may be extended to interactions in other settings and to the group's overall recognition of women's exclusive control of certain types of organizational activities.[11]

The Legion of Mary, or Legio Maria, began as an offshoot of the Catholic lay organization by the same name. Its origin in East Africa dates from 1963. By the early 1970s, the group was estimated to have a membership of more than 90,000, primarily within the Luo ethnic group in Kenya and Tanzania. A Luo woman, Gaudencia Aoko, joined the Catholic Legion of Mary. In 1963, two of Aoko's children fell seriously ill after an accident that she attributed to sorcery. As a result of this incident, Aoko began a religious crusade and established her own antiwitchcraft movement that ultimately broke away from the Legio. She sought the assistance of a self-styled prophet, Marcellanius Orongo, a Luo from Tanzania, and was baptized by him.

Crucifix and rosary in hand, Aoko healed the sick, burned amulets, and battled against alien spirits.[12] Aoko's group promised cure of chronic diseases and release from sorcery. Her example inspired Luo women by introducing the possibility of freedom from the domination of their husbands and in-laws, a continual source of tension and frustration in Luo society. In encouraging these reforms, Aoko's movement reacted to the political structure of the Catholic Church and developed a lay clergy with married priests and priestesses. Nonetheless, Aoko's appeal was short-lived. As her following began to decline, Aoko was unable to establish a stable church community, and her influence did not spread to the outlying Tanzanian branches of the Legio. The problem of female leadership and succession again appears to have been one of inability to transform ceremonial influence into an official position of full-time leadership and to transfer that leadership from women of one generation to those of another.

The examples above have been drawn from new churches that are independent of mission organizations rather than from separatist movements that have evolved from mission Christian churches. Because separatist movements involve a direct break from mission control, one might expect that they, too, would emphasize influential roles for women in reaction to the limited roles held by lay African women in mission organizations. To a certain extent, this is exemplified by Aoko.

The Power Struggle Between the Sexes: Themes of Women's Leadership in African Churches

The symbolic domains of men's and women's activities are clearly demarcated in contemporary African religious groups. In some cases this demarcation has resulted in a virtual separation of gender-linked activities and secrecy with regard to the social distribution of power between the sexes. Thus men may be the holders of important religious symbols and knowledge to which women have no access, and the same holds true for women. The secret societies and spirit cults of West Africa are prototypical cases of such separation.[13] In these cases, represented by the Sande, or Bundu, secret society in West Africa, separation allows women to wield autonomous ceremonial authority. Separation, however, creates an autonomous sphere of influence for women's activities. A similar situation characterizes independent churches in southern Africa that emphasize healing. Healing activities pertaining to women are a separate domain of expertise and influence in these groups. Through these activities, women have attempted to change the balance of power in the social order and to alleviate their physical and emotional suffering. Thus they have attempted to fulfill the first three of the four wishes I have listed.

Of the approximately 3,000 indigenous churches currently in South Africa, three quarters are churches that are based on spiritual healing and the charismatic powers of their leaders.[14] These churches are classified as Zionist and trace their origins to John Alexander Dowie's American evangelical church established in Zion City, Illinois. The concept of Zion represents utopian spiritual liberation that is shared by a number of churches, which are labeled either Zionist or apostolic in central and southern Africa. Geoffrey Parrinder elaborates on this definition of independent churches in South Africa:

> The churches which Sundkler calls Zion are akin to the prophetic and healing churches of other parts of Africa. They call themselves Zion, Apostolic, Pentecostal, Faith, and so on. They seem to have been inspired by a Zion church in Illinois which taught divine healing, triple immersion, and the near second advent of Christ.[15]

Thus independent churches of the Zionist or apostolic type may be considered under a single category. Members of both types of churches emphasize the relationship of divine healing to spiritual revelations and testimony. Churches of the apostolic type, including the Apostles of John Maranke and the Apostles of John Masowe, both originating in Zimbabwe, emphasize healing as a manifestation of spiritual redemption.

Bryan Wilson emphasizes that healing is a common theme in new African religions. He summarizes:

The demand for thaumaturgy . . . is endemic, and especially so in societies in which medical and religious practice are closely identified, and in which a wide range of worldly activities require the reoccurrence of supernatural goodwill.[16]

According to Wilson, even revolutionist and millenarian movements resort to healing as a theme when other means of expression prove ineffective. The association between healing and nurture makes this activity a common domain for religious expression among women in African churches. As already indicated, these women often assume the roles of healers, midwives, prophets, and spirit mediums. Activities that are socially associated with women become symbolically linked to them on the spiritual level, and this linkage is the basis for women's ceremonial leadership in the new African churches.

This connection is not peculiar to African churches. In another context Rita Gross writes:

This solution to the problem of women and their religious role is often connected to . . . women's maternal experience. Those who find the key to solving the problem of women's religious life in this area of concern tend to be advocates of the thesis that the maternal function is the primary source of women's social value and of their inner fulfillment.[17]

When considering the new African churches, this perspective may not be dismissed easily because it has deep cultural implications. Women often identify with these religious movements by using a maternal-healing metaphor, and they join for reasons associated with their nurturant roles as wives and mothers.

Women in these apostolic groups hold the positions of prophets and healers. Among the Maranke apostles, all women are considered potential spiritual healers, and most women hold the confirmed office of healer. *Burapi,* or spiritual healing power, is the focus of their ceremonial activities. Although healing is defined as an inspired act for which one must be especially gifted, it is also the most basic of all spiritual concerns for the Maranke apostles.[18] Maranke members refer to their organization as "a church of healing and prophecy." All other forms of spiritual exercise, including baptism and evangelism, are considered to contain elements of healing. In the absence of an official healer, other members routinely perform these duties. When women in one Maranke congregation protested against this overlap in male and female ceremonial functions, they were informed that the most active and spiritually powerful members of the congregation could heal. Thus, although healing is the only ceremonial activity that is available to most women, it is considered to be within the domain of expertise of all influential male members as well.

There are several types of women healers among the Maranke apostles: healer-prophets *(baprofiti mapipi),* "ordained" healers *(marapi),* and midwives. All operate with the basic assumption that there are no "natural" illnesses. Evil actions and demons are believed to cause sickness. Spiritual laxity, manifested through anger or transgression of food taboos, allows demon possession to occur. The possibility of possession is always present. Baptism, which cleanses the new member and symbolically reinforces personal conversion experiences, is accompanied by a comparable vulnerability. Healers and exorcists help to protect the member. The *mapipi* specialize in diagnosing illnesses and often develop a reputation for their proposed cures. Similarly, the activities of the midwives are charismatic, involving hearing the mother's confessions, medical diagnosis, and delivery of the child.

Routine healers, on the other hand, are instructed in a brief healing ceremony that is performed after the weekly worship service or when requested. The majority of these women healers confine their activities to the domestic arena. In fact, women are encouraged to begin practicing their healing activities within their own families, particularly in caring for their husbands and young children. J.D.Y. Peel has noted similar patterns among Aladura, or spirit-type, churches in Nigeria.[19]

The centrality of healing and the limited identification of women with it in churches of the apostolic type suggest an ambivalence surrounding the images of women in these groups. Women may wield extensive ceremonial control in domains traditionally associated with domestic activities but are limited in their access to leadership in broader religious arenas. The source of ceremonial leadership in spirit-type churches is considered external to the woman herself. If she is a prophet or a spirit medium, she speaks on behalf of a spiritual force and can criticize the male leadership of the organization on these grounds. Healing is viewed as a "gift of the spirit," which, although linked to the social and cultural status of the woman, originates from a higher source.

The requirement of virginity for young women in some apostolic groups operates to define their collective roles while isolating these women from others. The "virgin ideal" has obvious Christian roots.[20] Therefore, it is not surprising to find it in new Christian-based movements in Africa. This ideal also has roots in traditional practices surrounding female virginity in many African ethnic groups. However, in the new religions the virgin status implies further social and ritual practices. Among the Apostles of John Maranke, a virginity examination *(mushecho)* is performed annually on all young women between the ages of eleven and seventeen. Those young women who pass ideally have the free choice of their future husbands. Those who fail are given away involuntarily in arranged polygynous marriages. Virginity reinforces group endogamy and the social control of young women while simultaneously helping the church members to adopt new patterns of marriage selection. The marital ideal that is accepted is not a Western Christian model but, instead, an entirely new combination based on a concept of religious purity that is unique to the African independent churches.

The ceremonial roles of women among the Masowe apostles are similar to those of the Maranke churchwomen, and their political influence is largely indirect. However, early on, the prophet John Masowe established a special group of "sisters," young women who were dedicated exclusively to serving him through spiritual work. These women are particularly worthy of discussion because of the symbolic role of virginity in their ritual seclusion.

The young girls whom John Masowe had acquired as devoted disciples were referred to as his spiritual "wives."[21] Their duty was to sing at weekly ceremonies and baptisms. During his lifetime Masowe allowed some of the sisters to marry other men under special conditions. However, before his death he decreed that those sisters who had been with him as spiritual devotees should never marry again. Today the major congregations of the Masowe church have secluded living headquarters for the sisters. New young women continue to be given over to the spiritual cause by their families. Their movements and activities are watched closely. Only a few of the sisters are eventually allowed to marry. The sisters symbolize the spiritual purity of the Masowe church. The restrictions placed on their lives are used to reinforce a group ideal of perfection. Most women in the Masowe church are not subject to these strict regulations and do not have to demonstrate the same degree of religious commitment that the sisters do.

Some feminist scholars of religion have viewed these cultural assumptions and patterns as extensions of a "patriarchal mentality." For example, Janice Raymond attempts to develop a theory of spiritual and social "androgyny" in which she argues that sexual equality should be used as a guideline to redefine spiritual symbolism and erase gender stereotypes in "patriarchal" religions. She believes that these stereotypes are perpetuated by the "patriarchal mentality." It is difficult to apply such a Western-based approach to cross-cultural data.[22] Although Raymond's approach is somewhat narrow from an anthropological perspective, it suggests a common cross-cultural linkage between concepts of spirituality and gender roles. Anthropologist I. M. Lewis describes the cross-cultural importance of the metaphor of spiritual marriage and gender-linked imagery in a variety of cults that resemble the African spirit-type churches.[23] The act of possession is itself often equated with a spiritual union. For instance, among the Sidamo of Ethiopia, possessed men in the traditional cults are considered "horses" for the gods and women are termed "mules." The gods "speak" in a lesser fashion through women. The folk belief in the female water spirit known as *mami wata* or *mambo muntu* (snake person) in various African cults is another instance in which a union of men and women with spirit powers occurs. Beliefs in *mami wata* spirits and fear of possession by these demonic women are common in new African cults and churches.

The imagery linking spiritual union and possession may also be found in such diverse traditions as the classic Greek Delphic oracle, mystic Christianity, and Haitian voodoo. In the case of the African-based Christian churches, women prophets and healers are often viewed as agents of the Holy Spirit. Although not actually considered "possessed" by the spirit, these women are viewed as vehicles through which spiritual power is expressed. Women, thus, are seen as subordinate agents of higher supernatural and social forces. The uxorial bond with the supernatural force emphasizes the double symbolic subordination of women to both spiritual forces and men. Often spiritual subordination is expressed in cultural terms that reflect the existing patterns of domination and subordination that characterize daily social activities.

By the same token, women may use spiritual inspiration to reverse these everyday patterns through ritual events. For example, among the Maranke apostles, women who are not allowed to preach in church services, criticize male leaders through spiritually inspired, improvised songs. As long as they occur in the appropriate ceremonial context, these song-criticisms are tolerated by the male leaders. For a moment during the ceremony the social order is modified by an alternative religious reality.

The concept of spiritual union, the association of healing and nurture, and the virginity ideal are all gender-linked themes that recur in different ways in Africa's new religions. These themes define and isolate the social activities of women. Through these themes and the attendant social and ritual practices, women may exercise ceremonial leadership but are always circumscribed in their sphere of influence. They are called on to renounce certain traits associated with womanhood in order to achieve special symbolic roles. A complex patterning of dominance and subordination is at work in this type of gender-linked imagery. These patterns point to an ambivalence toward the cultural status of women as spiritual equals but social subordinates in the new religions. However, the cultural dynamics of the shift between daily social roles and ceremonial leadership are quite complex and cannot be explained away by theories of social domination. Instead, it is helpful to turn to women's accounts of their own experiences of conversion and membership in the new religious groups.

Conversion Experiences and Women's Participation

The participation of women in the new African religions relates directly to their accounts of the conversion experience. However, it is not possible to establish a simple cause-effect relationship between reasons for conversion and the extent of eventual participation by women. Women in both apostolic groups described earlier often join as a result of their husbands' involvement. The regulation of exogamy is an essential mechanism for maintaining group identity among the Maranke apostles. This reinforces the religious community as an insulated group that can be entered primarily through conversion. Women whose husbands are not members of the group are instructed to make every effort to convince their husbands to join. Young unmarried women are urged not to marry "pagans," including both traditional religionists and members of mission churches. Voluntary polygyny is permitted among the Maranke apostles and serves as a means of assuring group endogamy in a situation in which women outnumber men demographically.

As a result of these marriage practices, some women describe their conversion to membership with respect to domestic circumstances. Joining the church, in this instance, does not appear to be an independent personal choice but is instead related to women's compliance with familial expectations. The women who join to fulfill the wishes of their husbands and other relatives may be clearly distinguished from those who initially become involved through their own visionary or religious experiences. The first category tends to remain more passive after membership, whereas the latter group is more fully involved in ceremonial leadership.

My investigations revealed that regardless of the avowed motivations for joining, the explanations for conversion given by the Maranke women differed substantially from the benefits of membership that they perceived. One woman who admitted joining to follow suit with her husband and parents stated that she remained a member "to receive the hidden life of Christ" and the Holy Spirit's blessings. When this woman described her responsibilities in the church, she mentioned only "routine" healing. Many women stated that they questioned neither their conversion nor their spiritual gifts of healing, but merely expected them to be confirmed *because* they were women.

Three accounts, in particular, illustrate the differing conversion experiences of Maranke women. In the first case the woman felt pressured to join because of her husband's affiliation. She resisted membership for seven years, until a final confrontation occurred. She described the experience as follows:

While we were in the village, my husband became very ill with a stomach disease. The prophet said that he could be cured only if I were baptized. I agreed that the Apostles could baptize my body but they could not have my soul. When I approached the water and reluctantly entered it, a snake appeared out of nowhere. The baptist hit the snake and broke it in two pieces with his staff. I then said go ahead. Baptize both my soul and my body.[24]

This woman was subsequently confirmed as a healer and remained a committed, but not an active, member of the church. Although her husband was a leading evangelist and a special church judge, she did not attend a women's subgroup and song sessions. Her attendance at worship ceremonies was sporadic. Nevertheless, she was considered a member in good standing and a competent healer.

The second respondent was a prophet. She gave illness as her motivation for joining and stated emphatically that she had not joined through her husband's influence. She met regularly with a women's social group in the church and, as its only prophet, was considered its leader. Her participation in weekly ceremonies and in individual wilderness retreats was regular and active.

The third respondent, a healer, stressed the connection between a spiritual quest and physical healing. She stated that she had joined the group to seek a "hidden life in Christ" and to receive help in childbirth. She found relief from birth disorders through the church and proclaimed that, as a result of joining, she had given birth to six children without complications.

Many women gave pregnancy problems and childbirth as reasons for joining. Membership gave them access to the services of the Apostolic midwives. One woman stated that she had joined after losing her child in the seventh month of pregnancy. Another woman said that she had joined in order to cure a menstrual disorder that had caused continual bleeding that could not be cured through Western medicine. The latter informant recalled that for several years she had resisted her parents' request to join the church, viewing the new religion as incompatible with her high school education and secretarial training. However, complications resulting from the birth of her first child drew her to the church, although her husband remained a nonmember. She stated that her faith had increased through the "miracles" of healing that she had witnessed, and she found an active outlet for church life in her parents' family. In this case the parents' family and church activities also provided some escape from the duties of her own home.

A critical element leading to increased commitment seems to be active participation in either familial or women's prayer and social groupings surrounding the Sabbath worship service. Apostolic women who are involved in associational subgroupings seem to be more active in both worship and ceremonial leadership.[25] It is difficult to generalize about the transition from passivity to active membership of women who were forced to join the African churches. Nevertheless, the extent of a family's participation in the church seems to be an important aspect of a woman's conversion and membership experience. My observations suggest that the wives of elders are more assertive and directly involved in church activities than the women who participate neither in leadership through their husbands nor in women's associational subgroupings. Such women are, however, unable to function as co-owners of their husbands' positions in the absence of a grouping of women that is ready to respond to their leadership. They cannot develop an independent power base for their activities without the social support of other women.

Ritual Roles and Ceremonial Leadership

Women in the apostolic groups exercise most of their influence and leadership through ceremonial activities. Through singing in the weekly ceremony they compete with men to present the public moral messages that complement male sermons. Healing is a religious activity in which most Maranke apostolic women engage and may eventually lead to ceremonial authority. The virginity examination *(mushecho)*, midwifery, and certain types of healing exist as separate activities for women. In these cases, women derive their influence on the basis of rites of power that are independent of men's activities.

In the Maranke apostolic group, prophets hold roles of ceremonial leadership that transcend the domain of women's ritual activities. Even in this case, they are able to comment on and veto men's activities but not to generate their own projects. The influence of the prophet is based on her charismatic appeal and spiritually derived skills and does not involve the direct exercise of political decision making. For the Maranke apostles it is possible to distinguish between ceremonial leadership and expressive participation in terms of the following contrasting activities:

Ceremonial Leadership	*Expressive Participation*
Prophecy (includes formal rank)	Healing (includes formal rank)
Midwifery	Routine healing
Morality songs (women's sermons)	Songs of exorcism and healing
Virginity examination	Free choice of mate
Decision making for women's issues	Singing and prayer

These activities and similar rites are found in a variety of African spirit-type churches. Expressive participation in ceremonies may eventually translate into ceremonial leadership roles. However, in the case of healing and midwifery these roles are directed toward other women or domestic activities. The position of the prophet is broader but is based on a charismatic source. Although this portion of the analysis refers largely to the Maranke apostolic data, it also applies to the new religious groups discussed earlier in which women such as Mai Chaza and Lenshina achieved positions of spiritual leadership but were unable to transfer their roles to future generations or institutionalize the practice of female leadership.

Conclusions

The new African religions in which women have played a significant role are by-products of processes of rapid social change and development. Uprooted rural-urban migrants have found in these movements new networks for association and support. This has particularly been the case for women who, deprived of their previous productive economic roles in the countryside, have experienced underemployment and marginal social identities in the city.[26]

The new religious groups founded by women have emphasized the formation of utopian communities in which former productive domestic roles held by women can be reestablished or broadened. A parallel development may be noted in the recent appearance of neotraditional women's initiation rites in African urban areas.[27] These rites include the virginity examination in the Maranke church and modified forms of traditional clan and cult initiation ceremonies. Initiation rites in the modern context have served to reinforce the domestic roles of women but have not increased their political influence outside the home. Movements of religious protest have seldom developed into voluntary associations that directly influence the economic lives of women in the city.[28] They have, instead, reemphasized the integrity of conventional roles for women.[29]

Ceremonial leadership for women has, however, emerged as an important contribution of Africa's new religions both as an extension and as a reinterpretation of traditional forms of spirit mediumship and women's influence. In some cases, this form of leadership is accompanied by rights of office or is supplemented by limited political leadership. In other cases, it is replaced by expressive participation through which women exercise some influence over ceremonies. The new religious order may thus actually overturn accepted social arrangements that exist outside the religious domain.

Ethnographic and historical data indicate that women's leadership in the new African religions has been precarious and short-lived. However, case study materials drawn from the Maranke apostles suggest that participation in their own subgroupings leads women to have a sense of efficacy and to use collective interactions to redefine their positions in the religious community. The next step in such research is to begin to compare information about household structure, the economic autonomy of women, and child-rearing practices with accepted social ideals. This comparative information could become the basis for assessing how the sources of women's leadership roles and self-assertiveness in the religious domain reflect and influence their activities in other social contexts.

The examples I have presented suggest that women in Africa's contemporary religious movements have difficulties in redefining family structure and collective action to meet their new ideals. These problems have contributed to the marked contrast between ceremonial leadership, which often remains ephemeral or limited to a particular context, and experiences of masses of women as rank and file members of Africa's new religious movements. As prophets and symbols of ritual purity, many of these women are recipients of positions of symbolic privilege without political power.

The cultural ambivalence that is characteristic of women's roles in the new African churches refers to the tension between their unique ceremonial positions and their social and political roles. The religious ideals held by and about women in these groups often conflict with their actual exercise of power in daily life and church decision making. For example, Maranke apostles pride themselves on improving the lot of women by advocating the abolition of brideprice and the free selection of marital partners within the group. However, these practices are accompanied by voluntary polygyny and the continuation of arranged marriages with "informal" bridewealth exchanges. Moreover, women have little say in modifying any of these practices.

If the new African religions are considered to contain cultural forms and symbols in transition, we may view the ambivalence toward the position of women as one aspect of this change. Women are considered the spiritual equals of men before God, and their social possibilities are modified by this symbolic imagery. However, these social possibilities are also restricted by accepted cultural conventions and by patterns of social control and dominance established in the group. In order to incorporate aspects of feminist theory of religion into a thorough cross-cultural study, it is necessary to differentiate between cultural imagery about women and the social reality in which they live. The apostolic prophet criticizes male leaders only in her spiritual role, not in her social role. The constraints of the social order limit the definition of the religious reality. In African cults and churches the four wishes discussed at the outset of this chapter are fulfilled on the levels of cultural imagery and ceremony but not in daily social practice. These wishes are cultural projections of a utopian ideal that may eventually be realized through religious practices that contradict accepted social conventions.[30] These religious ideals, however, cannot be viewed in isolation from the social and historical context in which women's subordination is a feature of survival in the modernizing world.

The position of women in the new African religious groups evidences a double social and symbolic dependency. Although the new religions purport to offer women members hope for change, the social and cultural impact of these movements on the status and daily lives of churchwomen remains to be seen. Unless the cycle of women's adepthood and participation in the new religions alters considerably, the pattern of short-lived leadership, most recently exemplified by the demise of Lenshina's movement and the transfer of Mai Chaza's authority away from women members, will undoubtedly be repeated in the future before a significant change occurs in the balance between ceremonial leadership and women's political power in Africa's new religions.

7

Third World Women and Men: Effects of Cultural Change on Interpretation of Scripture

Constance F. Parvey

Rapid changes the world over—in political and economic structures, in law, and in the family—continue to challenge conventional patterns and symbols of male/female roles in both First and Third Worlds, in capitalist and in socialist countries. Christian women—in dialogue with one another and with men—are sifting and winnowing, claiming the present time and unearthing from the church's theological past those signs of hope that can inform and motivate new community for women and men in church and society. "We have been called to live in society, to live, to suffer, to serve, and to share the message of God's salvation."[1] This chapter is an expedition in spirituality for a changing church. It is not about history or culture but about revelation, about how the Holy Spirit is addressing Christians today with the fresh wind of the Word of God.

Between Old Myths and New Images

Transitions and shifts in society prompt new reflection about the church. For women, the church has always been a place for service; the church itself is most often symbolized as a servant people. But today, women the world over are asking what it means to be a servant of Christ in rapidly changing social contexts. They are asking if serving is the same for those who serve involuntarily as for those who are free to decide what service needs to be done and how to do it. For women, the decision to become a servant of Christ has usually meant that only certain types of spiritual models and roles would be open, those given in the past to women by men, and under male authority. Christian women are struggling as they reexamine the church's teaching in light of their being full persons, participating beyond the ascribed limits of sex-linked status, reaching for equal partnership with men in following Christ into a renewed spirituality.

As part of this seeking, women are breaking out from age-old patterns of "the woman's place"; they are reexamining old reference points about "the nature of woman." Caught between old myths and new images, women are beginning to find a spirituality that is based on scripture yet open to relationships of mutual responsibility among women and men for the decisions that govern their lives, that meet new needs and visions of ministry and servanthood for this time.

I say this from the perspective of having directed a special program of the World Council of Churches called "The Community of Women and Men in the Church Study" from 1978 to 1982. The purpose of this study was to explore these changing roles of women and men the world over. Its goal was to deepen the church's understanding of these changes and of their impact, present and potential, on the church's understanding of itself, its teachings and ministries. To enable this process, a thirty-two-page booklet was designed for use among the more than one hundred WCC member churches. Questions in the booklet ranged from those of identity, relationships, and life-styles to those of scripture, theology, ministry, and church structures. Local groups in churches, ecumenical councils, seminaries, and churchwomen's organizations the world over undertook the study. These local groups were then followed up by six regional meetings, held between 1978 and 1981. These meetings took place in cities as diverse as Bangalore, India; Ibadan, Nigeria; San José, Costa Rica; Beirut, Lebanon; Stony Point, New York; and Bad Segeberg, West Germany. The participation of women and men at each regional meeting was about 60 percent women and 40 percent men. The entire study process culminated in an international conference held in Sheffield, England, in July 1981, gathering together from among the thousands of groups that had participated in the study about 250 persons from ninety member churches of the World Council of Churches, delegates from fifty-five countries.[2] This was the first time in the history of the WCC, and perhaps in the history of the church, that so many women and men gathered to talk about partnership as a theological issue, with implications for the functioning of the church itself, particularly its teachings about interpretations of scripture and their negative and positive impact on women. The diversity and commonality of the issues that were raised touched people profoundly—spiritually, intellectually, and personally.

Each regional consultation lifted up its own special concerns. The overriding issue for Europeans was peace and the necessity for women to be engaged in curbing the acceleration of the nuclear arms race. Passion for peace was also a main concern of the Middle East consultation. Although that consultation took place during a breathing period in the war, from time to time one could still hear the shelling on the Beirut streets. Participants in both meetings knew from experience how much women and children suffer when war destroys life and destabilizes the fundamental institutions and services required for human and cultural survival. The North American meeting was marked by debate over inclusive language and issues of social justice, particularly the need for new models of community across barriers of race, class, and sex. Participants in the Latin-American meeting looked at their situation of double oppression: first, oppression by militarism and by the multinational corporations that dominate their economies and, second, the oppression of women by men through a strong macho tradition. The Asian consultation shared these concerns of double domination with its impact on the poorest of the poor and the extreme misery of women and children in countries in which much land is rich and a small elite are incredibly prosperous. In Africa the concerns centered around the community and the family, the tension between autonomy and life with/for others. In this context Christian attitudes toward polygamy were discussed, as were those of the ethics of celibacy. Their overriding issue was how to find ways within African tradition to reconstruct a Christian life and ethics that could be Christian and at the same time appropriate to African cultural integrity.[3]

Receiving and Rediscovering Scripture

There is much talk today about how scripture should be interpreted. But there is another question that is much neglected: How is scripture received? What impact does scripture and its authority have on the lives of those who have become Christians in non-Western contexts?

We have to begin with the fact that scripture has been received in Third World cultures after many centuries of accrued experience in Western culture with its historical evolution and many subcultures. In the case of Asia and Africa, large areas of these diverse peoples had had no prior contact with Christianity before the missionary movement of the past century. This does not mean that Christians were not present. There have been churches in Ethiopia and India, perhaps since apostolic times. However, cultures in Africa and Asia have been shaped mainly by the religious influences of Hinduism, Buddhism, Islam, and other indigenous religions. These had a powerful impact on the life of the people before the nineteenth-century missionary movement. A starting point for Christians in the Third World is how scripture has been received by them in relation to their own indigenous cultural contexts as well as the value systems that Western culture brought along with its interpretation of the biblical message.

With respect to women, the impact of Christian missionary preaching resulted in either establishing or reinforcing the subordination of women. Such passages as Genesis 2 and 1 Corinthians 11 and 14 were used frequently: the former to establish women's subordinate role—Eve as second to Adam—and the latter to establish the subordinate position of women in the church through the command that they be silent (1 Cor. 11) and keep their heads covered (1 Cor. 14).

Women in the churches of the Third World, parallel with women in Western churches, have been making their own conscious reflection on the roles that they have received and accepted as authoritative. They are doing their own assessing as to whether or not the Bible has been truthfully interpreted in relation to their identity. They are asking, is it indeed the case that being a Christian woman is synonymous with being a subordinated and subservient person? Being aware of structures of domination, oppression, and exploitation in other areas of their lives, they are awakened to what sexually defined structures of domination and oppression have done to women and how this made the situation even worse, particularly for women who are poor and do not have the protection of family wealth, social status, or education.

Looking at the negative impact of subordinationist teachings and servitude is not all that Third World women are doing. To stop there could mean to dismiss scripture and perhaps also to give up Christianity as well, regarding it ultimately as a faith that does not give women a fair and equal chance. Rather, women are saying that it is not the Bible that is wrong; the underlying problem is the false interpretation of scripture and its improper use and application. Consequently, they are turning their energies to an investigation of what the Bible actually says about the equality of women and men and their equal empowerment in God's work of creation and redemption. In doing so they are discovering that this is not a minor biblical theme, but a major one that transcends many ages and cultures over thousands of years of biblical history. They are discovering that the Bible actually begins and ends with an affirmation of the equal partnership. This means that women and men in churches of the Third World are beginning to sort out what they have received from the West about the Bible and see how it differs from what the Bible actually says. In this revisioning they are seeing how the Bible actually speaks to them directly, not first filtered through Western culture and its attitudes toward women.

The following two accounts of this process are from the Asian and African regional meetings of the Community Study. In reporting what they have said I have tried to be as faithful as possible to their words, their texts, their setting. I want to establish as direct a contact as I can between you, the reader, and the participants in these meetings, the first in Bangalore, India, and the other in Ibadan, Nigeria—cultures very different in almost every way, except that they share similar colonial and missionary histories.

Scripture, Culture, and Caste

The Asian Consultation took place at the United Theological College in Bangalore, India, in August 1978. Present at the four-day meeting were sixty-five delegates representing the major denominations of India (Protestant, Roman Catholic, and Orthodox) and a number of churchwomen's organizations and seminaries. A few participants came from Thailand and Sri Lanka. The large assembly hall in which we met was plain and functional. The room took on color and excitement with the splendid array of cotton and silk saris worn by the women delegates.

For Christians in India the cultural impact of the caste structure on both church and society is a major unsolved concern, a source of gross injustice in many ways. Every Indian is born into a caste, and the status of individuals or families has traditionally been determined by the status of the castes to which they belong. Generally overlapping and reinforcing, but sometimes competing with this older hierarchy based on birth, is the more recent class hierarchy based on wealth, education, and power. That women have become at best pawns and at worst victims of the struggle for status within these hierarchies can best be seen by a brief examination of the joint family and the dowry systems—the latter being the social evil that was mentioned most frequently at the consultation. Dowry traditionally was the share of the family inheritance that was given to a daughter at the time of her marriage in lieu of any claims on the family property. Today it is the price that the bride's family pays to the groom's family in order to get a "good match" for their daughter, the amount varying according to the status of the families involved and the groom's potential income. It is supposed to help assure good treatment of the bride within her new joint family, and as a high-caste custom,[4] it also functions as an attractive status symbol for aspiring families.

The joint family is patriarchal and usually patrilineal. An important part of its purpose is to keep the family together and to preserve the family property from one generation to the next. The joint family is controlled financially by the groom's father and older brothers. It is controlled domestically by the groom's mother. In the joint family, the wife leaves her home and enters permanently the household of her husband. She becomes legally and economically his property, and socially within her new family she is under the authority of her mother-in-law.

This means that, on entering marriage, no matter what the woman's caste—from Brahmin to untouchable—she has few, if any, legal rights within the household. The poorer the woman and the family, the more she is likely to be powerless and even severely maltreated. Modernization has modified the joint family system, most notably in the urban areas, and the Indian Constitution guarantees the equality of women and men, but even so, these long-established attitudes of the family system still work to discriminate against the majority of women. This includes not only the dowry system, which demeans women, but also inheritance rights and educational opportunities, where sons are favored over daughters.

The consultation at Bangalore pointed out that regardless of the religion—Hindu, Muslim, or Christian—religious ideology has served to reinforce the attitudes of the patrilineal family system that subjugate women. This combination of caste and family patterns makes the situation of the poorest women extremely vulnerable. Within the family she may be a kind of family slave or outside the family she may be used as a commodity of exchange, exploited for sexual privileges to placate moneylenders and landowners. According to one of the consultation speakers, Mrs. V. M. Chandran,

> The final degradation of our tradition and culture is the extension of dowry to all caste groups, which makes her [woman] feel a liability. In many areas, the silent majority of men still remain unawakened to this injustice.[5]

The consultation urged the churches to work to overthrow the injustices of dowry and seek to give women their equal rights in marriage.

Mrs. Chandran linked the cultural issues of women's inferiority to the church's use of scripture.

> Even the missions which established Churches in this country . . . handed down to us a tradition of women's inferior role. Wrong interpretations about the "true nature of the woman," her "intrinsic gifts," the "mission given to her by God," have made men and even many women blind to discrimination and injustice practised on women. . . . The Church which has always proclaimed loudly the freedom and dignity of all human beings has all along been dominated by the Hebrew Christian tradition that the subordinate role of women is the order of creation.[6]

It is wrong, she said, to assume that in the order of creation God established "the superordination of man and subordination of women to be fixed for eternity."[7]

Leelamma Athyal, in one of the morning devotions, also pointed to the misuse of Genesis 2 as a religious justification of women's subordination.

Lord, they say that according to the creation story, woman is made out of man; therefore, she is subordinate to him. They forget that the same creation story says that man was formed out of the ground, yet nobody will argue that man is subordinate to the ground. Another argument is that man is made first and then Eve; therefore, woman is inferior to man. Lord, how would you like it if someone says that you created animals first and then man, and so man is inferior to animals?[8]

Mrs. Athyal's point is that the scripture has been distorted by a male tradition of interpreters and that this reinforces what is already a male bias in the culture. She maintained that both the tradition of Christianity that India inherited and its own indigenous Indian culture must be renewed if the true message of the gospel is to be recovered. Only through this kind of conversion of the Christian community in terms of the Indian cultural context will women be able to overcome their internalized and socialized submissiveness. Only then will women be able to participate freely in the decisions regarding their lives, including their choices about marriage partners, their rights in the workplace, their values and experiences in the financial management of the family and in the education of their daughters.

Dr. J. Russell Chandran, principal of the United Theological College in Bangalore and husband of Mrs. V. C. Chandran, underlined the importance of redressing these scripturally based injustices against women in family and social life.

The quest for the authentic human community is still going on. What we have in reality is a distortion of the community brought about by exploitation and oppression. The tradition of male domination has influenced the interpretation of scripture, theology and ecclesiastical structures. Both man and woman need to be liberated from such distortion so that they can realise their genuine humanity.[9]

Despite modernization and the breaking down of the joint family, the consultation did not argue for the nuclear family as an alternative, nor did they argue for individualistic rights. In their handling of Genesis 1:27–28, the passage about being made in God's image, they interpreted it not in terms of the creation of individuals, nor the creation of the first man (male), but as the mutual and equal creation of men and women within communal life. They had no difficulty with the text that clearly states that in the image of God, "male and female he created them."

They maintained that sexual differences are two expressions of the one corporate life. Thus sexual identity itself informs us that God intends us not to be isolated individuals, but to be with others in community; this is built into the very nature of creation. The dimension of our being male or female is part of our common personhood. The report understands being created in the image of God as a process to be achieved, a "flower-ing," a growing in community in God's image. However, this growing has been obstructed by the Fall (Gen. 3). We have put a hindrance between our lives and God's intention for us. This is what we call sin. Often considered the starting point, sin is not the foundation of woman/man relationships, but the sign of its distortion.

The consultation did not argue for the maintenance of the status quo of the Fall, of the broken community. Rather, it argued for the re-creation of the human community, of male and female, "flowering in the image of God." The emphasis was not on the grand and glorious creation of the individual; rather, the assumption was that part of the very nature of being a complete person is to live in community, as a member of the body. The arguments against dowry and against subordinationist atti-tudes in the joint family were part of the searching in scripture for new foundations for community and family life based on the Word of God itself, and not on cultural or sex-biased interpretations of it.

As Christians have received the gospel in their own cultural settings, and as they are more and more aware of how much Western interpreta-tion of scripture lies hidden in the way they have received it, they are particularly sensitive to the sociocultural context in which scripture is interpreted, whether it be in the setting of the faithful people of ancient Canaan or modern Calcutta. This was evident in the comments made about 1 Corinthians 11, whereby women have been asked to be silent in the congregation. Dr. P. Victor Premsager, principal of the Andhra Christian Theological College, stressed how important it is to understand scripture not as a rule book of truths, but as God's Word dynamically revealed in the everyday happenings of life.

> We need not blame Paul for what he did not intend. His epistles were written for particular local churches having in view the local problems, cultural and social customs and practices. We have to study the scriptures in terms of the specific problems that they faced, the struggles they had to undergo in being faithful to their Lord, but not make them rules of conduct for today. St. Paul himself seems to have been afraid that people might misuse this advice and take it as the word of the Lord (1 Cor. 7:25).[10]

For participants at this consultation the equality of women and men in church and society is understood as both a theological and spiritual issue. Because of sin the relationship of "being one flesh" is broken. The task of the Christian community is to heal this distortion and alienation of women and men from each other and bring them to their authentic identity in interdependence and mutuality. This has to begin by listening to the voice of scripture in a different way.

The report warns, however, that in a hierarchical society that is characterized by extreme disparity in caste and class, it is not enough that middle-class churches grant equality to middle-class women. This is not what the gospel is about. Mrs. Jyotsna Chatterji who works with poor women in the rural areas made clear that "women's struggle for equality must be related to and form a part of the common struggle of women and men for social justice and transformation of society."[11]

In other words, equality is not for the privileged; it calls for a servant church. In revisioning servanthood, Mary was offered as one such model for the church. It was pointed out that the correct translation of Mary's reply to the angel is not "handmaiden," but "servant." "Handmaiden" points directly to the sex of the person, but servant does not. Moreover, the report stated that the word "servant" is the same term used by Isaiah and Jesus; thus "the functions of Mary, Isaiah, and Jesus were similar and should be beyond sex. They were all servants of the Lord."[12] Embedded in this comment is a strong criticism of both ecclesiastical structures and social stratifications shaped by caste and class. Mary is not a model for subordinating women in the social hierarchy, nor is she a model virgin goddess, an unattainable ideal. Mary is the model of the church as a community of those who freely choose to serve, women and men who make themselves totally available to be servants of God, joined in community, sharing their many and abundant gifts in truth and love as Christ has shown the way. The report ends with these words of commission: "We were reminded of St. Paul's call to the Christians in Rome not to be conformed to this world, but to be transformed. . . . We heard the call of God in these words."[13]

Scripture, Culture, and Identity

The African Regional Consultation was held at the Center for Church and Society in Ibadan, Nigeria, in September 1980. Ibadan was just recovering from devastating floods—removing the debris and mourning its dead. Into this setting, thirty-one official participants arrived from eleven African countries. About an equal number of women and men were daily visitors from the Ibadan area. They represented a range of churches from the Salvation Army to Baptist to Anglican and Roman Catholic. French, English, and Spanish translations were used to enable people coming from countries of differing colonial histories to communicate with one another.

Africa is a continent of many indigenous cultures, overlaid with a long history of colonial and modern involvements. The question was posed: What role does scripture play in establishing a Christian identity that is both authentically Christian and authentically African?

One of the findings of the African regional meeting was that much of traditional African culture that is negative toward women is reinforced by direct transfer to Old Testament stories. They pointed particularly to Genesis 2 and 3, the story of Eve's creation out of the rib of Adam and the story of the Fall, their eating of the forbidden fruit. The conference reported that Genesis 2 is most often used to argue for women's second place or inferior status. This has had its impact on all women, but particularly on the poorest women—those who are illiterate and often in poor health and who spend their days cooking, caring for children, carrying water long distances, and collecting firewood, any of which in itself is a full day's task. Subordinated status adds a cruel burden to what is already a desperate life circumstance.

Alternative interpretations were sought. The participants maintained for Genesis 2, the creation of Adam and Eve, that since man was created from mud and woman from man, woman must therefore be not inferior, but superior, since the material of man is mud, but the material that makes woman is human life itself.[14] They also argued that "bone of my bones and flesh of my flesh" (Gen. 2:23) must mean that women and men are equal; male and female become one flesh. In the same story they also challenged the interpretation of the word "helper." Why, they asked, should a helper be considered a person in an inferior position when we go to teachers, doctors, and many other people in highly respected social positions for "help." We regard these people as helpers, as equals, as perhaps superior in some areas. They then began to ask who has decided that being a "helper" is an inferior work when even the psalmists and prophets speak of God as "our helper." They felt that to define a "helper" as inferior points to the root of the cultural problem of biblical interpretation. Being subordinated was not part of the original theological meaning of "helper."[15] It is a distortion imposed on the text based on the values of a particular culture.

Zula Sofola, a Nigerian playwright and speaker at the consultation, showed how language itself is not neutral or innocent, but carries cultural biases. She demonstrated how European ideas about woman are linguistically derivative from those about man and how this European linguistic problem influenced the Western interpretations of scripture that Africa, in turn, inherited. For example, she pointed out that in English there is no neutral word that can mean either man or woman. With the exception of words like child, baby, and infant, all the others —male/female, mankind, humankind, man/woman—have a male root. She contrasted this to two of her own African languages, Ibo and Yoruba, in which this is not the case. In Ibo she showed how the root word for male and female is child, *Nwa,* making *Nwaoke* (male) and *Nwa-anyi* (female), and in Yoruba the root is *rin,* making *okunrin* (male) and *obinrin* (female).[16] Whereas in English the linguistic symbols for woman are symbolically subordinate, in these two African languages, as in others, this is not the case. It is therefore essential, she argued, that African women and men work directly with scripture, drawing on their own languages and cultures and not transposing the cultural attitudes of European Christians on African Christians. Sofola underscored the need for Africans to seek their own identity in scripture vis-à-vis their own cultural realities and languages.

Like the Asian counterpart, the African consultation also saw the importance of Genesis 1:27–28: "That God created humankind in God's image, male and female God created them." The equality of women and men is established here at the beginning of scripture. It is not until the Fall, in Genesis 3, that they noted, "We see differences in roles."[17] It is not as a result of Creation, but as a result of the Fall that the man, Adam, becomes the tiller of the soil and the woman, Eve, becomes the mother of life and sufferer in childbirth.[18] In Genesis 1, man and woman have the same mission; in Genesis 3, role differentiation is imposed. This, they argued, continued until the crucifixion, when they stated, "Jesus through his death . . . took all curses away."[19]

But questions still lingered regarding the Pauline statements about women in the church, especially 1 Corinthians 11 and 14, the first of which exhorts the women to keep their heads covered, usually interpreted as meaning they are subordinated, and the second, which admonished them to be quiet in the assembly and, if they have questions, to wait until they get home and then ask their husbands. Although no definitive answers were given, there was a general sense that these texts were situation specific, related to concrete problems at particular times and not meant to be general rules. What interested the consultation more was why it is that these two texts are so often used to justify the subordination of women yet no one ever preaches about Galatians 3:26, 28: "In Christ . . . there is neither Jew nor Greek, there is neither slave nor free, there is neither male nor female; for you are all one in Christ Jesus."

> Few people have ever heard a sermon on this passage. It has been more or less ignored by the male-dominated church. This passage which stresses the equality in Christ and specifically includes the relationship between women and men is a genuine transmission of the good news. In the relationship of God with us, we are the chosen people, women and men, rich and poor, etc. We are part of God and together with God in Christ. This is the kind of partnership we are meant to have in the church.[20]

Their overriding image for God was that of God being present in the Body of Christ. One participant spoke for many in saying:

> As I struggle with what the church is, I start with the concept of the Body of Christ. In the Bible there are many images. Jesus came and announced the

coming of the Kingdom from his own village, interpreting God's Kingdom in terms of concrete social responsibility. The Yahwehist movement, before him, carried the theme of God's judgment as something that happens in time: This is the Day. Jesus went out and selected the Twelve; they were concrete people. I want to be an active participant in this continuing concrete Body of Christ. This makes me wonder about the Eucharist. It is not something soft and easy. The Eucharist is food for heroes.[21]

The Old Testament story of Sarah and Hagar was discussed as a notable expression of oppression. Members of the consultation pointed out that not only did Sarah oppress Hagar, but Abraham also oppressed Sarah by denying that she was his wife (Gen. 20:2ff.). In other words, women oppress women and men oppress women, and as a consequence, some women end up at the bottom of the pyramid. This negative impact of the social hierarchy was countered, however, with stories of Old Testament heroic women who provided new models. Among the women mentioned were Miriam, the sister of Moses who dared to confront her powerful brother; Deborah, the commander of the army; and Hulda, the prophet. King Josiah had to listen to Hulda "for it was through her wisdom that the destiny of Judah was revealed."[22]

Counter to the Fall and the sequence of Abrahamic stories, the lives of these exceptional women evidenced a much larger role for women in scripture, a role, they felt, was later diminished.

> The attitude of Jesus to both women and men was the same. He went beyond the culture of his day. He healed Peter's mother-in-law and the woman with the issues of blood, same as the man with paralysis (Luke 4:38–39, 8:43–48). He commended many for finding time to listen to the Good News (Luke 10:38–42). He took account of women who did not count. Read the widow's mite in Luke 21:1–4. He showed interest in the underdog and the downtrodden, e.g., the Samaritan woman (John 4:7–30). Christ appeared first to a woman after his resurrection (John 20:1–18). Compare this to the list of people who Jesus appeared to in 1 Cor. 15:3–8. Women were not mentioned. This is a clear indication that women might have featured prominently in N. T. times but incidences which they were involved in were omitted.[23]

Behind this view of the participation of women in ancient Israel and in the early church is their experience with the role of women in religious movements, not only in African indigenous religious groups, in which a priestess tradition still exists, but also in Christianity as it began in Africa. Many women were involved in the early missionary movement, as missionaries from abroad, as local founders of churches, and as key leaders in the building of African Christian life. Consequently, this consultation assumed that women were also integral, in their numbers and in their leadership, in the founding of the first Christian communities. "Almost every new religious movement is ushered in by women, before men took over the leadership of it, e.g., Christianity. Women were to start preaching the story of the resurrection (Luke 24:9–10; John 20:18)."[24]

In asking themselves why the church has interpreted scripture as it has, in particular the assigning of subordinate roles to women, the conference located two problem areas. First, the Bible as a whole is not well known in Africa and is not preached as a total witness of God's purpose; rather, "the Bible is read too much in isolation, and some texts are preached on over and over again while others are left out."[25] And second, the "teachings of Scripture are not related to the local life of the people."[26]

The challenges of scripture and identity for African women and men have been overlaid with Western interpretations of the Bible on top of the problem of choosing isolated texts. The participants saw as their task the need to rediscover the biblical message as a whole in dynamic tension with traditional and modern African culture and its needs in order to bring together a new configuration, a new envisioning of the reality of God's equally created partnership of women and men. This meant that the images used for God were also to be reexamined.

The report continued, "The image of God confined in one's mind depends on one's cultural background. Since human beings have physical limitations, it is inevitable that in order to grasp the concept of God, He/She has to be anthropomorphised."[27] They gave examples out of African tradition of male and female symbols for God. From Douala in Cameroon, one participant said, "In Akan tradition, God is always spoken of as 'He'; in Ga language, the name of God is sometimes *Akaa Maa Nyogmo*—Father/Mother God." They compared this with the Hebrew *Elohim,* a word that combines *Eloh,* the name of the female goddess, and *im,* a Hebrew masculine plural ending.[28]

In a manner similar to that of the Asian meeting, the African women saw the vision of the church as a body in the attention given to family and community. Although they acknowledged many problems with the extended family, they did not view the nuclear family as an alternative. Rather, they argued for the extended family's positive values. "There is security and help in counseling members of the family, help in bringing up the children, and in sharing of the burdens of others. It is important to keep the extended family system working. Modern society works against it and there are insufficient systems in the church to support, sustain, and encourage the wider family."[29] As one section of the report put it: "We can learn from African religion [how] the tradition of eating from one bowl united people."[30]

A litany during the celebration of Holy Communion, presided over by the Reverend Margaret Boama-Secu, a Presbyterian minister from

Ghana, and Sister Marie-Madeline Handy, founder of a women's religious community in Cameroon, summarized and symbolized through its inclusiveness the spirituality of "eating from one bowl."

WOMEN: By faith the disciples of Jesus proclaimed: "The Lord has risen indeed, and has appeared to Simon."

MEN: By faith Mary Magdalene proclaimed, "I have seen the risen Lord."

COMMUNITY: We praise you, Lord; because you live, we shall live also.

LEADER: Almighty God, you built your church on the rock of human faith and trust.[31]

In this litany the man, Simon Peter, has a woman partner on "the rock of human faith and trust." Her name is Mary Magdalene. This vision of the church as a new community of women and men is a vision of the shared weaknesses and strengths, the fallenness of human persons and the effectiveness of God's redemptive work symbolized in the Marys and the Peters, those who make up the new community in Christ transforming the curse of Eve and Adam.

In their own words:

> Adam and Eve shared the first paradise,
> And today man and woman both share
> The joy and sorrow,
> The courage and fear,
> The faith and uncertainty,
> The hope and the despair.[32]

Cultural Change Means Going Back to the Sources

Leaping across cultures, what is transparent in these two accounts is a convergence of Christian tradition and women's tradition in interpreting scripture, striving for continuity and integrity amid enormous diversity. Women's tradition, as a self-conscious movement, is new in the churches. There have always been women in the church, women teaching in the Sunday schools, serving in the altar guild, and working in pioneering areas as missionaries, teachers, healing ministers, and social workers. Women have served the church and have been used by the churches, but their own experience has not been counted as equal with that of men and certainly not as equal with that of the clergy, an office from which women have been mostly excluded. Women are turning to scripture to learn what reasons have been used against their equal and full participation. They can accept cultural reasons why this has not been done in the past, but with radically changed and changing cultural situations, they are asking what grounds there could be for maintaining this exclusion. This is only one of the many new questions that Christian women are bringing to the Bible today. As a consequence, they are exposing themselves to more of scripture, and they are finding more of themselves in it, more empowerment as equals with men in the image of God, and more role models for ministry in the strong and courageous women of ancient and apostolic faith—prophets, founders, and hosts of congregations, and witnesses and proclaimers of the resurrection news.

Every movement for Christian renewal returns to the sources. This is clearly seen in the Reformation and in the tradition of reformers throughout the centuries of the church, whether it be Francis of Assisi, Brigid of Sweden, or Perpetua and Felicitas in second-century Rome. Women in the Third World, like their sisters in the First, are taking the responsibility for interpreting the scripture in light of their own self-reliance, empowerment, and experience, not filtered through the eyes of male bias in their own cultures or through the eyes of those who have brought a culturally biased Christianity to them. Building on women's values and experience, they are affirming not only their own integrity but also the dignity of all those who have been considered subordinate. They are not only affirming their own freedom but also taking hold of their common responsibility with men to set all people free. They are not only envisioning and working toward their own partnership in community but are setting the value of the community itself over individualism, relationships over self-concentration, and transformation in community over domination, autonomy, or isolation.

To reflect theologically about scripture means to relate the Word of God to our own experience and time. Spiritual renewal is not just accepting what is given; it comes from a living, direct encounter between the message of the truth of the Word of God and the issues of our present situations. To hear it means to stand with those who have gone before, and to interpret it is to listen in each new place and age for that Word which is uniquely appropriate. The theological reflections of these Third World women and men represent a process of uncovering the image of God in cultures whose memory and social organization is vastly different from that of the First World. As a result, there is an incredible freshness and directness in their thought. Adding the dimension of cross-cultural experience to biblical interpretation strips all of us of our cultural pretensions. The Word of God becomes a countersign to our disunity, division, and distrust. Equality is discovered as a foundation of faith; it has been hidden from our eyes. Justice in community reappears because community is of fundamental importance. The Magnificat of Mary is revisited because there can be no ministry without those who freely choose to give and receive.

III
THE CHURCH AND THE STATUS
OF WOMEN

8

Women in Philippine
Basic Christian Communities

Mark Jeffery Ratkus, F.S.C.

This chapter seeks to determine whether the operation of Philippine Basic Christian Communities (BCCs)[1] has enhanced the image and role of Philippine women or in any way changed the social relations between the sexes. Drawing on solicited assessments about and personal observation of women in the BCCs of the rural Ilonggo-speaking sections of the country's western Visayan Islands region, and using published information to provide perspective and comparison,[2] the study concludes that although the BCCs have been successful in improving certain aspects of the welfare level of their members, they have not had an effect on the status of women as such because they have not set out explicitly to do so. This indicates that desirable change is likely to happen only through consistent and conscious planning.

Philippine Basic Christian Communities

Basic Christian Communities are shaped by theological factors and the salient socioeconomic conditions obtaining currently in the Philippines, conditions that the BCCs seek to ameliorate. Their nature, functioning, structure, and distinctiveness reflect a pastoral plan aimed at fostering total human development. Also, in that the BCCs represent an economically progressive but socially conservative movement, they provide a context within which the status of women in the Philippine BCCs may be appreciated.

The theological developments that led to the foundation of BCCs can be traced by examining official church pronouncements, such as John XXIII's *Pacem in Terris (Peace on Earth)* of 1963, in which he linked the demands of religious faith to efforts aimed at improving peoples' lot "both in the natural order as well as in the supernatural."[3] The Second

Vatican Council's *Pastoral Constitution on the Church in the Modern World (Gaudium et Spes)* extended this idea by contending that "reverence for man" requires ensuring the rights of people to food, clothing, education, employment, appropriate information, good reputation, conscience and privacy.[4] A further broadening of the church's teaching is evident in Paul VI's exhortation to world leaders to work for human, not just economic, growth. He argued that, in order to be authentic, economic growth had to "provide for the progress of each individual, and of the whole man."[5] That is, the benefits of economic growth extend beyond material improvement, and believers must work to see that these benefits are distributed equitably so that all people might have the opportunity to develop fully.

These statements document the church's gradual movement toward a more explicit commitment on behalf of the poor and oppressed, a commitment that the 1971 Synod of Bishops termed a "constitutive dimension of the preaching of the Gospel."[6] Hence, the church's members are not only to provide immediate aid to the victims of underdevelopment, but also to seek long-term solutions that will eradicate the causes of poverty and injustice. That this theological ferment in the church at large began having its effects in the Republic of the Philippines (RP) may be seen in the following paragraph from the Philippine Bishops' Pastoral for the First Sunday of Lent, 1983:

> Poverty is the economic condition of life in which the vast majority of our people live. Notwithstanding attempts at alleviation, it continues to grow more deeply. The structures built into the social system are at the root of this recalcitrance to change for the better. The government has initiated a massive program of economic development aimed at correcting problems of poverty. But a number of its key developmental priorities, like heavy reliance on multinationals and its favoring of their needs over those of the people, its attention to tourist facilities and services, like lavish film festivals, over the services it can and should provide to rural areas, do not appear to lessen the number of our poor, which is growing daily—their destitution more acute.[7]

Two important points emerge from this statement. First, it is implicit that the contemporary Philippines is beset by massive poverty, disease, illiteracy, unemployment, and various sorts of inequality.[8] The second is that the bishops mean to evangelize the poor both by direct dealings with them and by appropriate criticism of those governmental practices and policies that serve to buttress the status quo.

The Rise of Basic Christian Communities

Although this writer's main source of information is the parish of Oringao, in the municipality of Kabankalan, Southern Negros Occidental in the RP's western Visayan Islands region, reports from other parts of the Philippines suggest that the structure, functioning, and effects of the BCCs in this parish are fairly similar to those located elsewhere in the republic.

The current formal structure of the BCCs in Negros evolved over the years through the trial and error process of seeking to meet the felt needs of the people, a process begun initially in 1967, when the Reverend Niall O'Brien, S.S.C., an Irish Columban priest, founded Sa-Maria House as a retreat and seminar center for the development of barrio (village) leaders. Seminars were offered on community organization, labor unionization, legal aid, self-help for tenant farmers, and self-awareness.[9]

Besides these outreach programs, Father O'Brien instituted a live-in farm project that gradually took on the appearance of a communally run agricultural kibbutz.[10] The communal experience benefited the members in many material ways and also enhanced their spiritual lives. Specifically, the prayer life of the group, since it had a greater opportunity to flow into and out of the members' shared life experiences, became more integrated with and less distinguishable from "everyday life." Consequently, it was quite natural that the hallmark of BCCs came to be the Panimbahon, which

> is essentially a priestless service with a fixed series of readings and prayers for use on Sundays and with strict rules of membership and attendance. Involving Bible reflection and community prayer, it is conducted by men from the neighborhood who meet as a prayer community at least once a week, often with the distribution of Holy Communion. In Kabankalan the *Panimbahon* spread to most of the barrios, and soon became the target of the military and political establishment in the area.[11]

Two aspects of the Panimbahon are worthy of comment because they reflect the purposes of the BCCs. First, the reflective reading of the scriptures and the members' sharing of its practical meaning for them individually and collectively provide the basis for the future direction of the group. Second, the service takes place without a priest, conducted by one of the group's trained members—a *kapillan*. These local liturgists are selected by the group, and the community pays the nominal "tuition" charged by the parish for the training seminars; this out-of-the-group-back-to-the-group dynamic has strengthened the communities' cohesion and self-reliance, and it is precisely this movement toward self-sufficiency that began to rankle the local political establishment. The *kapillan* post seems to be limited to men. Thus, although the BCCs are fomenting many changes (i.e., toward faith-based group action and toward group autonomy), certain aspects of social relations appear to have been left intact (e.g., the *kapillan* position as a male preserve).

In addition to the BCCs' being formulated to minister spiritually to the people, the communities are designed to assist in various aspects of human and communal development. For example, the Reverend Brian Gore, S.S.C., an Australian Columban, was appointed pastor of Oringao in 1977, and he proceeded immediately to educate people about their basic human rights, which traditionally had been trampled on by rich lowland families. Father Gore was also instrumental in organizing among the communities economic self-help projects, workshops on diagnosing common maladies and preparing herbal medicines, and seminars for improving agricultural technique.[12] The institution of the Konseho sang Kristyanong Katilingban (Council of the Basic Christian Communities) provided local BCC leaders with the chance to familiarize one another with common problems and to begin discussing solutions. Clearly, this echelon of organization enhanced cohesiveness both within individual communities and among them. Thus this multifaceted pastoral plan reflected the holism inherent in the theological developments discussed earlier.

A highly significant function of the BCCs is their contribution to the safety and security of their members. In the late 1970s there arose in southern Negros a crisis for members of the Kristyanong Katilingban (KK) in the form of the Salvatoris, a millennialist-religious group who were seeking to find the Promised Land in Mindanao. These people believed that their amulets protected them from bullets, and they proceeded to terrorize the hill people and seize their livestock.[13] On October 25, 1979, the Salvatoris killed a KK member in the mountainous area between Bulwang and Bulusan. This galvanized the communities to protect their members; in effect, they said, "We too know how to kill in self-defense." This stand prompted many outsiders to join the group, which now had credibility as an effective force with staying power. It also led many people to move their residences closer together for safety and to form rural barrios where there had been none. From this simple start the BCCs have in various ways fought injustices being perpetrated against their members, and they have supported the legal rights of their priests and lay leaders, who have been arrested more recently on specious murder charges.[14] Hence, although the promotion of safety was not an initial goal of the BCCs, it has come to occupy more prominence as the self-reliant cohesion of the KKs has elicited more strident opposition from those whose privileged social, economic, and political positions have been challenged.

The structure of the BCCs may be illustrated by the communities and by the work of Conrado Muhal, a married full-time church worker, who heads the educational program of the parish and who has been jailed for his activities:

The BCCs in Oringao are groups of 35 to 50 families living close together who study the Bible, pray and plan for development together. In the parish there are 52 BCCs. Muhal and the others in prison go from one BCC to the other, running seminars, teaching improved agricultural practices, settling the problems that arise between leaders and families.[15]

The fifty-two communities are clustered about eight centros (six or seven communities per centro), at which the Panimbahon, occasional Eucharists, and other meetings take place. Each centro has a president, vice-president, secretary-treasurer, and *kapillan,* and as noted, members of the parish team, like Muhal, visit the centros regularly. This practice sensitizes parish workers to the issues as experienced at the grass-roots level. Thus there appears to be between each BCC, its centro, and the parish team (comprising one priest and roughly twelve full-time lay workers) a constant two-way flow of information that helps to keep the parish programs relevant and vital.

The BCCs' rural location and especially their focus on integrated human development make them distinctive. The former point is important because two thirds of Filipinos live outside the cities, and the BCCs are the initial effort undertaken by the Catholic Church to evangelize and foster development simultaneously.[16] The latter is significant because little is happening "developmentally" in non-BCC barrios. Because church activities in these places are limited almost solely to devotional and liturgical practices, the levels of cohesion and participation in church-sponsored activities among residents in these places is virtually nonexistent in contrast to those that obtrude from the Kristyanong Katilingban. Despite stated government intentions to reach out to the nation's rural areas, the actual results of these on a large scale will occur only in the future, making the church's current efforts all the more crucial.[17] Aside from the BCCs, in many rural areas only the New People's Army, or NPA (the military wing of the Philippine Communist Party), works in the absence of government to keep order and foster development.[18] Although the NPA and the BCCs both exalt human dignity and share some agenda for reforms, the fundamental difference between them is that the BCCs' message is nonviolent and flows from a belief in God.[19] Therefore, the BCCs' uniqueness and importance lie in their emphasis on promoting human development that is total and integral and that takes place within a communitarian context.

The implicit assumption underlying the adoption of BCCs as a pastoral model is that all individuals within given communities would benefit from the programs conducted by the community or in the community by the parish. Specifically, from this writer's perspective there does not seem to have been any definite attempt to identify or address specific "women's issues" in the formulation of structures, programs, or activities. Similarly, at least at the outset, virtually no women were involved in the decisions about structure and function as the discussions proceeded on whether and how to adopt BCCs as a model, because these decisions were made largely by clergymen. Thus neither the content of BCC programs nor the process by which these were arrived at explicitly included women and their concerns. Thus the BCCs represent a plan that is economically progressive yet socially conservative.

Images and Roles of Philippine Women

A consideration of Philippine women in general and of Ilongga women of the western Visayan Islands in particular will help us to assess their status in light of the purpose of the BCCs. Then it seeks an answer to the question, what is the potential for changes in the status of women?

Overall, women in the Philippines are viewed primarily by men and by themselves as the hub of home life, and the characteristics they portray as well as the roles they play are generally congruent with this image. Sister Aloysia Albert, C.M., observes that this image prevails among the Visayan women to whom she ministers in Iloilo: "They still esteem that ideal woman of the home, of the family, the sweet and loving guardian, trying to make the wheels of life's chariot run smoothly."[20] Approximately 75 percent of rural women view their role as that of housekeepers; they work at least eight hours a day and at least twenty-nine days a month at this, their main activity. They often also perform family farm work and thus ordinarily have no time left for recreation or for dealings with outside issues.[21] Although 68 percent of rural survey respondents reported that they had observed women performing market work, "there is approval for mothers and wives working outside the home but mainly for financial reasons."[22] Other studies indicate that the rural Philippine woman's personality traits make her well suited to operating in an orbit that is static and limited almost solely to the home; she is described as being sensitive, emotional, thin-skinned, subjective, submissive, honest, dependent, and religious.[23]

The language used to depict the image of women in documents such as the statutes on inheritance would suggest that they are equal socially to men, as some observers contend.[24] Others, however, hold that various legal provisions taken as a whole see women as dependent homemakers and mothers.[25] This latter view, that women are less important or, at best, less in the forefront of society than men, seems to be more credible as one examines the data on sex differences of other studies that focus variously on diet, time spent working, and school attendance. For example, irrespective of age, males consume a larger percentage of their recommended daily protein and calorie intake than do females.[26] Similarly, men work fewer hours than women, except for limited periods of the agricultural cycle.[27] Additionally, beyond the elementary level of schooling, social and economic pressures to leave school are greater on females than on males, leading to a higher female attrition rate.[28] Clearly, all these elements of inequality between the sexes show that the current status of women is far from equal to that of men, and they also portend a bleak future for improvements in the welfare of women.[29]

Another area that reveals elements of the status of women is that of the decision-making pattern in family units. Women traditionally are the families' treasurers, and in the wealthier segments of society this role may extend to the acquisition and disposition of investable funds and other property.[30] Research has even shown that while in some instances women make the major political and economic decisions in families, they sponsor their brothers, sons, and nephews to hold political office rather than seek such positions for themselves.[31] This suggests an acquiescence to some social convention that overt leadership roles are ones that women are "not supposed to play," and it is even more likely that women would remain "behind the scenes" in poor or rural households; in families with these characteristics, "women exercise the greatest influence in matters relating to household chores, care of children, discipline of daughters and allocation of monetary resources."[32] This suggests that women are relegated to deciding on minor items only. Yet more research is needed on the significance of the content and impact of women's decision making, especially in rural areas.

With regard to decision making and the exercise of leadership, the Ilonggas of the western Visayans may be expected to be at least somewhat more assertive and prominent than other Philippine women for a variety of reasons. As early as 1663, for instance, Visayan women were categorized as "shrewd traders" of their handicrafts, and the 1970 census reports that rural women merchants outnumber men three to one.[33] Furthermore, 22.5 percent of Ilonggas are members of the Samahang Nayon, the national government's Village Cooperatives Program, a percentage that is second highest among the twelve regions; females also constitute 13.3 percent of leaders in the program, the highest percentage among the regions.[34] Other studies report the women of the western Visayans as being more likely to assume elected-official positions.[35] Thus, although women in general are expected to, and in fact do, confine themselves largely to the concerns and operations of their immediate households, Ilonggas have a bit more latitude to become involved in work or activities outside the home.

It is evident that the image and role of Philippine women confine them in large measure to working in and around the home, and although it is not the case inherently, women receive treatment inferior to that of men in a number of areas (e.g., quality of diet, hours worked, educational attainment). Thus the question arises, is the current status of women conducive to what BCCs hope to achieve? Because the data are fragmentary, the answer to this question must remain tentative.

Generally, there appears to be no dynamic within the current structure or functioning of the BCCs that would challenge the traditional image or role of women within rural Philippine society. That is, there is no reason to believe that women in the BCCs will suddenly reject the values associated with motherhood and working within the household. Because the BCCs strive to eradicate poverty and to promote human development within a communitarian context, it has simply been assumed that, if the entire group advances, all members of the community will experience an enhancement in the quality of their lives. Considering the degree of need obtaining in these rural communities, this assumption has proved thus far to be quite workable. More impetus for changes in women's status is likely to originate in response to deteriorating economic conditions in the Philippines. That is, as the purchasing power of the peso continues to shrink, the need for women to compensate for this by working for wages will become much more intense. Hence, economic factors, rather than anything connected directly to the principles of the BCCs, are likely to be responsible for precipitating changes in the roles that women play.

What has just been said about women's status overall cannot be maintained with regard to the overt inequalities to which women are subject. As more and more of the community's needs are met, the process of reflecting on the scriptures in the Panimbahon is bound to lead them to recognize and address the needs of women within the group. However, those expecting that this will be a quick process would do well to recall how long it took for believers to begin viewing slavery as inimical to Christian principles.

What is the potential for change in the status of Philippine women? Particularly for the Visayan Islands, a pertinent point that constrains any potential for change is the limited set of educational opportunities that are available. For example, among the western Visayan Islanders, 37.1 percent of the married women have received only primary schooling. When this figure is added to the number of those with no schooling, one can see that half the married women in the region are virtually illiterate. Similarly, the 11.2 percent of women in the western Visayans with a high school diploma ranks just above Bicol (11%), the lowest of all regions.[36] These statistics suggest that any change in women's status is unlikely to begin with women themselves, for few of them have had any opportunity to observe women functioning in nontraditional roles. Furthermore, uneducated women are simply unable to avail themselves of many new opportunities that do occur because they lack the skills that education attempts to develop.

Even the informal training provided by public and private agencies for poor rural women does not hold much hope for fostering change. In many cases, women are excluded from agricultural production training and from saving or investment programs despite the large amounts of time they devote to these or related activities.[37] Moreover, in the few programs that do target a female clientele, the efforts have been concentrated on sewing and cooking, thus further stereotyping the "appropriate roles" for women.[38]

Besides the lack of schooling, the hours spent working by women are so substantial as to preclude their significant participation in "development-oriented" activities, whether civic or church-sponsored. For example, one study reports women working an average of 72.5 hours a week, 58.4 hours of which is home production time (i.e., housework); 14.1 hours are devoted to market production.[39] Another study corroborated the average total hours figure among less wealthy families, wherein men worked 56.4 hours a week in contrast with the 73.2 hours a week for women.[40]

Although the foregoing points indicate that women in general face a difficult lot, the following observations for western Visayan women hint that the circumstances for housekeepers in this region may not be as severe:

> Less than half of the married women (48.8%) are involved in this activity at least 29 days a month (almost every day). This is the second lowest among the regions. This is also one of the regions with the lower proportion of women with activities besides their main activity (12% vs. 16.7% nationally). Twenty-three percent report work as their main activity, compared with the national mean of 25%. These figures indicate the potential of the married women of the Western Visayans for involvement in community activities other than housekeeping and work.[41]

Thus it appears that there exists some potential for change in the roles women play in the western Visayan Islands, although the same amount of leeway does not seem to obtain elsewhere in the country.

Because the extended family may provide child-care services and informal market employment opportunities may abound close to home, women need not sacrifice much wage work after having had a child; in economic terms the "opportunity cost" of childbearing is low if one defines cost as wage work and income foregone.[42] However, the cost in terms of women's leisure time extends throughout the child's preschool years. This way of defining opportunity cost "calls attention to a problem that must be addressed by anyone seeking to improve the welfare of women in developing countries: the drain on women's leisure caused by childbearing, particularly by repeated childbearing."[43] Because the "time devoted to children is responsible for differences in work time between the sexes," the availability of women for engaging in developmental projects is likely to be quite limited.[44] Hence the pattern of childbearing and the subsequent inequality of total time worked by women relative to that worked by men reflect the current image and role of women and serve to perpetuate that status into the future. Clearly, these issues are important in their own right and also because they set boundaries on the degree to which rural women can participate in civic or church-related programs for social and economic advancement.[45]

Summary

First, the Philippine woman's image and role place her in the nome as mother and manager, and this status appears to be quite viable in terms of the immediate goals of the BCCs. In other words, there seems to be nothing inconsistent with this status of women and the process of integrated human development that the Kristyanong Katilingban seeks to promote. Deteriorating economic conditions in the Philippines may make this role untenable in the future, but this force is distinct from the principles on which the BCCs are founded. Second, the potential for changes in women's status, although greater in the western Visayan Islands than in the republic's other regions, is quite circumscribed. Three factors combine to inhibit change: the low levels of educational opportunity and attainment among women, the high average of total hours worked weekly by women, and patterns of childbearing. Consequently, without a major redefinition of sex roles, women will not have the time to become involved intimately in developmental activities or programs. This is not to say that development efforts will be stymied entirely unless there is a prior change in women's status. It is clear, however, that women's concerns will not be addressed comprehensively as integral aspects of community development without first making their attainment explicit goals of the BCCs.

Women in the Philippine BCCs

When asked what roles women have played in the BCCs, Father Romeo Empestan, pastoral coordinator of sixteen parishes in southern Negros for the Diocese of Bacolod, replied that women work usually in the mothers' group health program as organizers and paramedical volunteers; they also organize sewing and vegetable-gardening classes and hog dispersal projects.[46] Father Rufino Suplido, chancellor of the Diocese of Bacolod, adds that, where public schools exist, women also catechize the children.[47] Thus the usual types of participation by women in the BCCs are very much related to their domestic roles (e.g., women demonstrating to other women how to be better mothers and housekeepers, or women teaching children).

Other women have assumed leadership capacities in the Kristyanong Katilingban as elected officers or they have been selected to be members of the educational team preparing couples either for marriage or for the baptism of their children. These roles are less traditional in that they are less connected to the domestic realm. The penchant for western Visayan women to take on leadership positions more readily than do other Philippine women may be reflected in the 20 percent of BCCs in southern Negros that have women leaders/officers, although, of course, it would be desirable to know also what percentage of BCC leaders are women.[48] Furthermore, one's effectiveness in active ministry depends on traits that transcend sex.

> The perceptible element is not whether a leader is male or female but the leader's commitment as manifested in her courage to continue in her work in spite of the risk of being picked up or "salvaged." It also depends on a leader's creativity to find means and methods of continuing their Bible Services amidst harassments.[49]

Evidently, the prerequisite for leaders to be effective is a faith that must be strong in the face of continual danger. Parenthetically, the word "salvaged," a uniquely Philippine usage, means that individuals disappear, and some time later their remains, often bearing marks of torture, are "found" by government patrols. This is but one of the types of harassment mentioned earlier, and it forms part of the context within which lay leaders minister to the rural poor. This perspective makes even more remarkable the degree of women's participation in leading the BCCs, and it reveals the fortitude these women possess along with their traditionally feminine traits.

It is now possible to assess how women have been benefited by the existence of BCC programs. Certainly, projects for economic self-help and medical well-being address some of the problems that rural women perceived in a 1975 survey as being important: employment, food production, capital, sanitation, road and school repairs, family planning, and nutrition.[50] These programs have been devised not only to help women but also to improve the quality of life for all in the communities of which these women are members. Another way to phrase this is that the programs aim to help women to function better in their present role rather than to change that role. It may also be that women have taken female BCC leaders as new role models, but this remains conjectural until more research is undertaken.

Three factors inhibiting changes in women's status were identified previously: low levels of educational opportunity or attainment, high average total hours worked per week, and patterns of childbearing. The KKs address only the first of these and, even this, indirectly. For example, the need to spend time on housework or wage work is cited most frequently by women as the cause for absenteeism or for dropping out of developmental activities or educational programs.[51] By conducting seminars and training sessions in the local barrios, instead of at some distance, the KKs raise the likelihood that women will be able to participate and to benefit educationally. As helpful as these programs may be, they often deal solely with women's needs within their current roles, and in any case, they are hardly an adequate substitute for sustained, formal education. The other two constraints on changes in the image and role of women remain in place, with no specific aspect of the BCC program to address either of them directly. Thus one is left to conclude that the BCCs' programs have not improved the status of women but have left it unchanged.

The traditional pattern of social relationships between the sexes is an issue that the BCCs have not questioned. Although few clear reasons for this are evident, it is likely that because the earliest planners were foreign, Catholic, male clergy, they were not in a position themselves to formulate such a question. Furthermore, in light of the Philippine woman's relatively retiring way of life, it is doubtful that the issue would have been raised even if women had been among the initial planners. It is also probable that the relationships *within* the communities were taken for granted, since one of the main reasons for the foundation of the BCCs was to ensure that the rural poor would be able to develop spiritually and materially despite the long history of oppression by the rich (i.e., by those *outside* the community). That is, the emphasis in the BCCs, particularly those in southern Negros, has been and remains their own cohesion in the face of strong opposition from the economically and politically powerful segments of Philippine society.

There are five additional questions that both BCCs and professional researchers need to consider in more detail. These questions are clearly relevant to the Philippine BCCs, and they are likely to be applicable anywhere that the enhancement of women's welfare and status is a priority item.

1. Are there aspects of the image and role of women that are inherently dysfunctional within the overall goals of the BCCs?

2. Presumably, the BCCs are seeking, as Paul VI put it, to "provide for the progress of each individual, and of the whole man." If the BCCs do not challenge the social inequalities and inequities experienced by women, how can they be said to be in agreement with Paul VI's point? What changes in BCC philosophy and goals would be necessary in order to address these inequalities and inequities directly?

3. What specific educational programs could BCCs provide for women to offset or remedy their lack of opportunity and attainment, and what is the optimal sequence of these?

4. In what ways might the time spent on child care be redistributed to allow women the opportunity to engage in other activities?

5. To the extent that childbearing patterns reflect and perpetuate the current role of women, which, if any, BCC-sponsored programs might modify these patterns?

Although the lack of fuller data makes the conclusion tentative, it is nonetheless evident that BCCs have not enhanced the status of women, because this aim has never been incorporated explicitly into the goal structure and policy formulation of the Kristyanong Katilingban. This is not to say that the BCCs have been ineffective, for there is ample evidence that communities as a whole have become more self-reliant, better developed economically and spiritually, and healthier. However, as has been the case in the economically developed, industrialized countries, the material progress of the society does not ensure that women will be treated equally or equitably. In order for such treatment to be attained, it must be sought explicitly.

An Annotated Bibliography on
The Church and Women in the Third World

Ellen Low Webster

T he church and women in the Third World is an important but
underdeveloped field of study. Women in most Third World countries have been impacted in a variety of ways by Christianity, a fact many
researchers on women tend to overlook. In like manner, researchers who
have written about churches in the Third World often ignore the fact that
women comprise half the churches' membership and have helped make
the churches what they are today. Perhaps a shared assumption that the
church is a male preserve unrelated to women is responsible for the
frequent and artificial separation of the stories of "the church" and of
"women." One consequence of this separation has been that scholarly
literature combining these two subjects is sparse, difficult to find, and
limited almost exclusively to article- rather than book-length studies.
This bibliography is an attempt to bring together recent empirical studies
on women and the church in the Third World in order to show what is
currently available in English.

In preparing the bibliography, I consulted *Religion Index One: Peri-
odicals, 1971–1983; Religion Index Two: Multi-Author Works, 1970–
1981; Bibliography of Asian Studies, 1977–1980;* and Clare B. Fischer,
Breaking Through: A Bibliography of Women and Religion (Graduate
Theological Union Library, 1980). References in the footnotes and bibli-
ographies provided in the books and articles listed here were followed
up. The research was carried out in the Burke Library of Union Theological Seminary, New York; the Lehman, Butler, and East Asian Libraries
of Columbia University; the Divinity Library of Yale University; and the
Rogers Library at the Maryknoll Sisters Center, Maryknoll, New York.
Although these libraries have comprehensive collections, they did not
have all the books and articles that I wanted to examine. This bibliography, therefore, cannot claim to be exhaustive.

The criteria used for the inclusion of articles in the bibliography were five in number. First, the articles had to be scholarly, not journalistic or impressionistic. It was sometimes difficult to make a decision on this, as some journalistic articles provided important information on subjects that have yet to be researched in a more rigorous manner. Second, the articles had to be empirical in focus. Thus, historical, sociological, and anthropological studies have been included, but not theological or ethical ones. Third, the studies, whether books or articles, had to be complete entities in themselves. Chapters or sections on the church and women in single-author works with a broader focus have not been included. Fourth, the articles had to deal with *women* in the Third World. Biographies of missionaries or of African, Asian, and/or Latin-American women were excluded so that the focus would be on the common experience of women rather than on the lives of exceptional women. Fifth, I was interested in recent research and so, with one exception, have not included works written before 1970.

The bibliography has been organized geographically according to region. The region most thoroughly studied to date is Africa. Over half the entries in the entire bibliography deal with eleven countries south of the Sahara. Of these studies on Africa, just under half are of Protestant churches, one quarter are of the Roman Catholic Church, and about one third are of independent or indigenous churches. A majority of those on indigenous churches are sociological studies based on field research, while many of those on the Protestant and Catholic churches are historical and based primarily on written mission sources.

One fourth of the studies in this bibliography deal with Asia, but only six countries in this region are represented. A mere seven articles are concerned with just four Latin-American countries: Mexico, Chile, Colombia, and Brazil. The studies of both Asia and Latin America are evenly divided between historical and sociological subjects. Only three of the Asia studies deal with Roman Catholics, whereas only one Latin-American study deals with Protestants.

In looking at the bibliography as a whole, one is struck by the fact that writing on this subject seems to be set within one or a combination of three different frameworks of inquiry. The first and most frequently utilized focuses upon women and assesses the significance of the findings in terms of what they tell us about women in various church situations. Within this frame of reference two themes dominate: the present position and role(s) of women in the churches under study and the influence which Christianity or missionary work and ideologies have had upon women, especially upon their social development and social status. The second framework of inquiry directs attention primarily to the church. While no one theme emerges from a comparison of those studies that fall exclusively into this category, those that combine the "church" and the "women" frameworks have as their major theme the contribution women have made to the development of the church. The third is an area studies framework the researcher uses to gain a deeper understanding of the culture and society of which both women and the church are a part. There were no common themes in the few studies in this category or those which combined this concern with either of the other two mentioned.

Although the annotations have to be brief, they should provide enough information to make the bibliography a useful resource for those who wish to study further, or even to do research, in this important field. Since their focus tends predominantly to be on the author's main thesis in relation to women, the annotations are set more often within the first framework of inquiry mentioned above than within the other two.

Africa

Breidenback, Paul. "The Woman on the Beach and the Man in the Bush: Leadership and Adepthood in the Twelve Apostles Movement in Ghana." In *The New Religions of Africa,* ed. by Bennetta Jules-Rosette (Ablex Publishing Corp., 1979), pp. 99–115.
    Drawing largely on interviews, Breidenback shows how the models of adepthood and leadership given by the movement's founders, John Nackabah and particularly Grace Tani, in their preaching and healing work have influenced women's current participation in this indigenous church movement.

Callaway, Helen. "Women in Yoruba Tradition and in the Cherubim and Seraphim Society." In *The History of Christianity in West Africa,* ed. by O. U. Kalu (London: Longman Group, 1980), pp. 321–332.
    Callaway draws parallels between the position and creative roles of women in the Cherubim and Seraphim Society of Nigeria and the Yoruba tradition, focusing particularly upon prophetesses and women's health problems.

Campbell, Penelope. "Presbyterian West Africa Missions: Women as Converts and Agents of Social Change." *Journal of Presbyterian History* 56 (Summer 1978), 121–132.
    Campbell shows how women converts in equatorial West Africa became the sustaining power in the indigenous mission churches and thereby agents of social change during the second half of the nineteenth century.

Gaitskell, Deborah. " 'Christian Compounds of Girls': Church Hostels for African Women in Johannesburg, 1907–1970." *Journal of Southern Africa Studies* 6 (October 1979), 44–69.

In this account of the creation, purposes, and demise of three church hostels, Gaitskell shows the missionary response to, and contradictory role in, the urbanization of single wage-earning African women, particularly domestic servants.

———. "Housewives, Maids, or Mothers: Some Contradictions of Domesticity for Christian Women in Johannesburg, 1903–1939." *Journal of African History* 24 (1983), 241–256.

Gaitskell shows how in the South African setting the ideology of domesticity taught by missionaries to African women was not only fraught with contradictions but also represented an ideal that was often impossible to achieve for economic and political reasons.

———. " 'Wailing for Purity': Prayer Unions, African Mothers, and Adolescent Daughters 1912–1940." In *Industrialization and Social Change in South Africa: African Class, Culture and Consciousness, 1870–1930,* ed. by S. Marks and R. Rathbone (London: Longman Group, 1982), pp. 338–357.

In her investigation of the historical origins and early developments of prayer unions in South Africa, Gaitskell shows the conflicts and problems that arose between mission Christianity and African society over the nature of maternal responsibilities in sex education.

Jules-Rosette, Bennetta. "Changing Aspects of Women's Initiation in Southern Africa: An Exploratory Study." *Canadian Journal of African Studies* 13:3 (1980), 389–405.

Field research in Zambia 1975–1977 is the basis for this comparison between traditional initiation practices and the *mushecho,* a women's purity rite, performed in the Maranke Church. Jules-Rosette sees the *mushecho* as both a reminder of custom and an indicator of change.

———. "Women as Ceremonial Leaders in an African Church: The Apostles of John Maranke." In *The New Religions of Africa,* ed. by Bennetta Jules-Rosette (Ablex Publishing Corp., 1979), pp. 127–144.

Jules-Rosette uses field work done in Zaire and Zambia in 1971–1972 to analyze female and male spheres of authority and to conclude that women's ceremonial leadership, based on healing-midwifery activities, does not challenge the traditional male hierarchical structure of the Maranke Church.

———. "Women in Indigenous African Cults and Churches." In *The Black Woman Cross-Culturally,* ed. by Filomina Chioma Steady (Schenkman Publishing Co., 1981), pp. 185–207.

Jules-Rosette discusses the various positions of women in the independent churches, such as founding leader, healer, singer, prophetess, and ordinary member, and suggests that these may be related to the difficulties women have had in redefining family and social organization.

Kirwen, Michael C. *African Widows: An Empirical Study of the Problems of Adapting Western Christian Teachings on Marriage to the Leviratic Custom for the Care of Widows in Four Rural African Societies* (Orbis Books, 1979).

Kirwen bases this study of the leviratic custom and the implications and results of the Catholic Church's prohibition of it on a sociological survey done in Tanzania in 1971–1972. He concludes that problems have arisen for widows and for the Catholic Church out of a failure to adapt Christian theology to non-Western cultural situations.

Kupalo, Ancilla. "African Sisters' Congregations: Realities of the Present Situation." In *Christianity in Independent Africa,* ed. by Richard Gray et al. (London: Rex Collings, 1978), pp. 122–135.

Kupalo presents current problems and needs of African sisters against the historical background of their congregations and suggests integrating African values into those underlying the vows of poverty, chastity, and obedience in order to make religious life more relevant and meaningful.

Lagerwerf, Leny. *"They Pray for You . . .": Independent Churches and Women in Botswana* (Leiden: Interuniversity Institute for Missiological and Ecumenical Research, 1982).

Based on field research done in Gaborone in 1977 and 1979, this case study focuses on the various roles of women, particularly that of healers, and the situation of unmarried mothers in some of the independent churches.

———. "Women in the Church: From Influence to Responsibility." *Exchange* 12 (December 1975), 2–79.

Lagerwerf uses books, conference reports, and papers to provide an overview of the present position and role of women in the churches in Africa, Asia, and Latin America. The longest sections deal with Africa and with religious sisters.

Mann, Kristin. "The Dangers of Dependence: Christian Marriage Among Elite Women in Lagos Colony, 1880–1915." *Journal of African History* 24 (1983), 37–56.

Mann discusses why elite women favored Christian to Yoruba marriage, the problems they experienced in trying to conform to foreign marital norms, and their consequent reconsideration of the conjugal roles.

Murray, Jocelyn. "The Church Missionary Society and the 'Female Circumcision' Issue in Kenya 1929–1932." *Journal of Religion in Africa* 8 (1976), 92–104.

This study focuses on the different approaches of two neighboring CMS mission stations to female circumcision, the response of the people affected by those policies, and the results achieved in abolishing the practice.

Muzorewa, Farai David. "Through Prayer to Action: The Rukwadzano Women of Rhodesia." In *Themes in the Christian History of Central Africa,* ed. by T. O. Ranger and John Weller (University of California Press, 1975), pp. 256–268.

This historical overview shows how the Rukwadzano rweWadzimai (Women's Fellowship) of the United Methodist Church, founded in 1929, has adapted to a rapidly changing society with the potential to become a formidable religious force within it.

Odwyoye, Mercy Amoa. "Standing on Both Feet: Education and Leadership Training for Women in the Methodist Church, Nigeria." *Ecumenical Review* 30 (January 1981), 60–71.

Odwyoye describes the women's work of the Wesleyan Methodist Missionary Society from the 1870s through the 1930s as a means of understanding present views on women's participation in the ministry of the church.

"Religious Life for Women in Zaire." *Pro Mundi Vita: Dossiers* (May 1980), 1–31.

After a useful historical introduction, this dossier reviews the Kinshasa Colloquium, August 15–21, 1979, at which forty-five Zairian sisters examined such areas of concern in religious life as image, renewal, formation, contextualization, life-style, future roles, and work.

Robins, Catherine. "Conversion, Life Crises, and Stability Among Women in the East African Revival." In *The New Religions of Africa,* ed. by Bennetta Jules-Rosette (Ablex Publishing Corp., 1979), pp. 185–202.

Robins uses interviews as primary data for describing the experience of and analyzing the reasons underlying the conversion of Kiga and Hima women in Uganda in the 1940s.

Spencer, Leon P. "Defence and Protection of Converts: Kenya Missions and the Inheritance of Christian Widows, 1912–1931." *Journal of Religion in Africa* 5 (1973), 107–127.

Spencer shows that in their petitions to government concerning the inheritance of widows the Kenya missions promoted individual rights and their own interests over against tribal rights and customs.

Steady, Filomina Chioma. "Protestant Women's Associations in Freetown, Sierra Leone." In *Women in Africa: Studies in Social and Economic Change,* ed. by Nancy J. Hafkin and Edna G. Bay (Stanford University Press, 1976), pp. 213–237.

Using her 1970–1971 field research, Steady argues that Protestant women's associations promoted a conservative ideology, not social change, and suggests that unification of all Christian women's associations might lead to a new female consciousness oriented to change.

———. "The Role of Women in the Churches in Freetown, Sierra Leone." In *Christianity in Independent Africa,* ed. by Richard Gray et al. (London: Rex Collings, 1978), pp. 151–163.

This is a shorter version of the above which concentrates on the role played by Creole women in fostering certain Christian values in their religious associations and the relations of these associations to the social structure.

Swantz, Marja-Lusa. "Church and the Changing Role of Women in Tanzania." In *Christianity in Independent Africa,* ed. by Richard Gray et al. (London: Rex Collings, 1978), pp. 136–150.

Swantz affirms the church's positive role in opening up new opportunities for women, discusses its negative role in helping to keep women subjugated, and suggests that it address women's current problems by working for structural changes in society.

Walker, Sheila S. "Women in the Harrist Movement." In *The New Religions of Africa,* ed. by Bennetta Jules-Rosette (Ablex Publishing Corp., 1979), pp. 87–97.

Walker uses the Deima Church of Marie Lalou in Ivory Coast to show that, although based on traditional social structure, the Harrist Church gave women a sense of new possibilities and new horizons.

Weinrich, Mary Aquina. "A Sociological Study of a Religious Congregation of African Sisters in Rhodesia." *Social Compass* 14:1 (1967), 3–32.

This study is a history of the Little Sisters of the Child Jesus and an analysis, based on a 1962 survey, of African sisters' social background, their reasons for entering the religious life, and their position vis-à-vis European missionaries and their African communities and families.

———. "An Aspect of the Development of the Religious Life in Rhodesia." In *Themes in the Christian History of Central Africa,* ed. by T. O. Ranger and John Weller (University of California Press, 1975), pp. 218–237.

The history of European and African religious congregations from 1889 to 1971 and the replies to a questionnaire from a small percentage of African and European sisters are the bases of Sister Mary Aquina's argument for the current need for women's contemplative communities.

Yates, Barbara. "Church, State, and Education in Belgian Africa: Implications for Contemporary Third World Women." In *Women's Education in the Third World: Comparative Perspectives,* ed. by Gail P. Kelly and Carolyn M. Elliott (State University of New York Press, 1982), pp. 127–151.

> This is a history of the sex-differentiated colonial educational system in the Belgian Congo from 1879 to 1920. Yates discusses the educational, social, economic, and occupational implications of this system for women.

Asia

Bennett, Adrian A. "Doing More Than They Intended: Southern Methodist Women in China, 1879–1898." In *Women in New Worlds,* vol. 2, ed. by Rosemary Skinner Keller et al. (Abingdon Press, 1982), pp. 249–267.

> Bennett discusses the work of the China Mission of the Missionary Society of the Methodist Episcopal Church, South, and concludes that its many facets, including cultural imperialism, contributed to the emergence of Chinese women as agents of social and political change.

Bradshaw, Sue. "Catholic Sisters in China: An Effort to Raise the Status of Women." In *Women in China: Current Directions in Historical Scholarship,* ed. by Richard W. Guisso and Stanley Johannesen (Philo Press, 1981), pp. 201–213.

> The work and fate of the sisters of four American congregations as well as of the sisters in the Chinese congregations they established between 1920 and the 1950s is the focus of Bradshaw's study.

———. "Religious Women in China: An Understanding of Indigenization." *The Catholic Historical Review* 68 (January 1982), 28–45.

> Bradshaw looks at the work of foreign and Chinese women, especially religious sisters and the founding of congregations, in an effort to assess the contribution they made to the development of an indigenous church in China.

Drucker, Alison R. "The Influence of Western Women on the Anti-Footbinding Movement 1840–1911." In *Women in China: Current Directions in Historical Scholarship,* ed. by Richard W. Guisso and Stanley Johannesen (Philo Press, 1981), pp. 179–199.

> Drucker uses the example of their pioneering role in the anti–footbinding movement to argue that the contribution of Western women, especially missionaries, to the struggle to raise the status of Chinese women was a significant one.

Forman, Charles W. " 'Sing to the Lord a New Song': Women in the Churches of Oceania." In *Rethinking Women's Roles: Perspectives from the Pacific,* ed. by Denise O'Brien and Sharon W. Tiffany (University of California Press, 1984).

Forman examines the history of women's changing roles, especially in decision making, in the churches in Oceania from the mid-nineteenth century to the present. He attributes current changes to global patterns rather than to indigenous influences.

Garrett, Shirley S. "Sisters All: Feminism and the American Women's Missionary Movement." In *Missionary Ideologies in the Imperialist Era: 1880–1920,* ed. by Torben Christensen and William R. Hutchison (Arhus: Aros, 1982), pp. 221–230.

Garrett analyzes missionary feminist ideology, which contributed to the growth and expanding role of women's missionary societies in America but which threatened deeply rooted cultural beliefs abroad. Examples are given of educational work in Japan and China.

Ihromi, T. Omas. "Social and Cultural Background of Concepts of Roles of Women: Reflections on the Indonesian Scene." *Ecumenical Review* 27 (October 1975), 357–365.

Ihromi describes the influence of family structures and inheritance laws on the position of women in various matrilineal, patrilineal, and bilateral ethnic cultures and shows that Christianity has produced change in marriage practices, educational opportunities, and roles for women.

Lee, Hyo-chae. "Protestant Missionary Work and Enlightenment of Korean Women." *Korea Journal* 17 (November 1977), 33–50.

Through an analysis of the work and methods of women missionaries, Lee examines the affirmative and negative ways Christianity affected the social development and status of Korean women.

Moses, Jane, and Grace Aaron. "Thirty Years of the C.S.I. Order for Women." *The South India Churchman,* January 1980, pp. 8–9.

A concise history of the Church of South India's Order for Women from its inception, written by two of the original sisters.

Paul, Glendora B. "Presbyterian Missionaries and the Women of India in the Nineteenth Century." *Journal of Presbyterian History* 62 (Fall 1984), 230–236.

By setting her study of Presbyterian "women's work" in the context of the social patterns and cultural norms affecting nineteenth-century Indian women, Paul shows how Presbyterians contributed to changing both their status and attitudes toward them.

Tellis-Nayak, Jessie. "Christian Women in India." In *Women in India and in the Church,* ed. by Engelbert Zeitler et al. (Indore: Divine Word Publications, 1978), pp. 199–211.

This overview of contemporary Christian women's contribution to the church and society in India gives primary attention to Roman Catholic laywomen.

Webster, Ellen Purdy. "Some Aspects of the Religiosity of Punjabi Christian Girls: A Sociological Study." *Bulletin of the Christian Institute of Sikh Studies* 5 (July 1976), 2–23.

This study is based on thirty-three interviews about what Christianity as a religious ideology means to girls in the Punjab (India) and whether or not it acts as a change-producing force in their lives.

Latin America

Flora, Cornelia B. "Pentecostal Women in Colombia." *Journal of Interamerican Studies and World Affairs* 17 (November 1975), 411–425.

Catholic and Pentecostal ideologies, organizational structures, and secular behavioral patterns relating to the status of working-class women are contrasted and conclusions made about Pentecostalism as an agent of change.

Gallagher, Ann Miriam. "The Indian Nuns of Mexico City's Monasterio of Corpus Christi, 1724–1821." In *Latin American Women: Historical Perspectives,* ed. by Asunción Lavrin (Greenwood Press, 1978), pp. 150–172.

Using a private collection of manuscript sources, Gallagher looks at the Indian nuns of Corpus Christi in regard to family background, education, services to society, reasons for choosing the religious life, and reasons for emphasizing the racial purity of their members.

Gilfeather, Katherine Anne. "The Changing Role of Women in the Catholic Church in Chile." *Journal for the Scientific Study of Religion* 16 (March 1977), 39–54.

Gilfeather shows how the expansion of women's roles in the pastoral and administrative work of the Catholic Church in Chile is changing their status, religious ideology, and cultural attitudes.

———. "Women Religious, the Poor, and the Institutional Church in Chile." In *Churches and Politics in Latin America,* ed. by Daniel H. Levine (Sage Publications, 1979), pp. 198–224.

This study examines the experiences of Catholic sisters living, working, and identifying with the poor in order to evaluate the consequences of these actions for their own lives and for the Chilean church as a whole.

Lavrin, Asunción. "Values and Meaning of Monastic Life for Nuns in Colonial Mexico." *Catholic Historical Review* 58 (October 1972), 367–387.

Lavrin looks at the values of monastic life as expressed in the vows and social background of the nuns. She concludes that the convents were, with a few exceptions, elitist, traditional, contemplative, and static in character.

————. "Women in Convents: Their Economic and Social Role in Colonial Mexico." In *Liberating Women's History: Theoretical and Critical Essays,* ed. by Berenice A. Carroll (University of Illinois Press, 1976), pp. 250–277.

In this survey Lavrin shows how feminine orders in the eighteenth century not only reflected and catered to the needs of the social elite but also influenced and participated in New Spain's economic development.

Soeiro, Susan A. "The Feminine Orders in Colonial Bahia, Brazil: Economic, Social, and Demographic Implications, 1677–1800." In *Latin American Women: Historical Perspectives,* ed. by Asunción Lavrin (Greenwood Press, 1978), pp. 173–197.

Soeiro explores the reasons for the belated founding of the four convents in Brazil, discusses their social composition and purpose, and suggests that the nunneries upheld the established patriarchal social order by removing from society women whose circumstances diverged from the sanctioned models.

List of Contributors

Beatriz Melano Couch holds degrees from the University of Buenos Aires and Princeton Theological Seminary and received her doctor of philosophy and theology degree from the University of Strasbourg, France, in 1975. She is currently Professor of Systematic Theology at Union Theological Seminary, Buenos Aires. She has lectured in the United States, Latin America, Asia, and Europe on topics pertaining to Latin-American liberation theology and the role of women in the church and in society. In addition, she has contributed chapters to many books, published numerous articles in Spanish and English, and is the author of *Hermenutica Metódica* and *Del Existencialismo a la Filosofía del Lenguaje.*

Stella Faria, until recently a general secretary of the Council of Catholic Women of India, is a graduate of Bangalore University and has an M.A. in political science from Mysore University, as well as a diploma in journalism from the Bharatya Vidya Bhawan. She is a co-editor and contributor to *The Emerging Christian Woman: Church and Society Perspectives.* In addition, she is treasurer of the Indian Council of Social Welfare, Karnataka branch, a member of the Executive Committee of the National Advisory Council to the Catholic Bishops' Conference of India, and an executive member of the Ecumenical Christian Center, Whitefield.

Shirley S. Garrett holds a doctorate in Chinese history from Harvard University. She is the author of "Sisters All: Feminism and the American Women's Missionary Movement," in *Missionary Ideologies in the Imperialist Era: 1880–1920,* ed. by Torben Christensen and William R. Hutchison. Her other publications include *Social Reformers in Urban China* and contributing authorship to *The Chinese City Between Two Worlds* and *The Missionary Enterprise in China and America.*

Katherine Gilfeather, M.M., received her B.E. in education from Rogers College, Maryknoll, and her M.A. in sociology from Columbia University. She went to Chile in 1955 and since 1967 has been a member of a research team at Centro Bellarmino, Santiago. Her publications include six studies in Spanish published by the Center, as well as articles in the *Journal for the Scientific Study of Religion* and the *Journal of Interamerican Studies and World Affairs.*

Bennetta Jules-Rosette is Associate Professor and Chairperson in the Department of Sociology at the University of California, San Diego. Her major research focuses on the new African religions, urban migration, urban employment in the informal sector, and women in development. Since 1979 she has conducted a series of field studies in Zaire, Zambia, the Ivory Coast, and Kenya sponsored by the National Science Foundation and the National Endowment for the Humanities. Her major books include *African Apostles: A Paradigm for Looking, The New Religions of Africa,* and *Symbols of Change.*

Constance F. Parvey, Research Scholar at the Wellesley College Center for Research on Women and Roian Fleck Resident-in-Religion at Bryn Mawr College, is formerly director of the Study on the Community of Women and Men in the Church in the Commission on Faith and Order of the World Council of Churches. She is a pastor in the Lutheran Church of America and before working in Geneva, Switzerland, she served as Lutheran chaplain at Harvard University and at the Massachusetts Institute of Technology and as pastor at University Lutheran Church in Cambridge, Massachusetts. She is author of numerous articles and author or editor of several books, including *Come Lord Jesus, Come Quickly; The Community of Women and Men in the Church;* and *Ordination of Women in Ecumenical Perspective.*

Mark Jeffery Ratkus, F.S.C., is a graduate of La Salle College and holds a doctorate from the University of Notre Dame. At present he is Assistant Professor of Economics at La Salle University, Philadelphia. During 1979–81 he taught at La Salle College, Bacolod City, Republic of the Philippines, where he studied firsthand the Basic Christian Communities of Southern Negros Occidental. He is an active member of the Association for Asian Studies and maintains a scholarly interest in Third World economic development in general and in Philippine development in particular.

Ellen Low Webster, a graduate of Connecticut College, lived in India from 1960 to 1981. A missionary of the Presbyterian Church (U.S.A.), she wrote and lectured on the role of women in the church and in society, as well as taught with her husband a course on "The Church and

Women" at United Theological College, Bangalore. She is the coauthor of "Teaching Indian Seminarians About the Church and Women" in *The Emerging Christian Woman: Church and Society Perspectives;* author of "Some Aspects of the Religiosity of Punjabi Christian Girls: A Sociological Study"; and contributor to *Good News for Women.*

John C. B. Webster, former Professor of History of Christianity at United Theological College in Bangalore, India, is currently pastor of the Waterford United Presbyterian Church, Waterford, Connecticut, and lecturer in Ecumenics and World Christianity at Union Theological Seminary, New York. He holds a doctoral degree in South Asia Regional Studies from the University of Pennsylvania and has published widely in the field of Indian church history. He is the author of *The Christian Community and Change in Nineteenth-Century North India* and recently served as guest editor of a special issue of *The Journal of Presbyterian History* on "Presbyterians in India/Pakistan" (1984).

Notes

Introduction: John C. B. Webster

1. Constance F. Parvey, ed., *The Community of Women and Men in the Church* (Fortress Press, 1983), p. 48.

2. Betty Thompson, *A Chance to Change: Women and Men in the Church* (Fortress Press, 1982), p. 72.

3. Parvey, op. cit., pp. 96–97.

4. Virginia Fabella and Sergio Torres, eds., *Irruption of the Third World: Challenge to Theology* (Orbis Books, 1983), pp. xvi–xvii, 247.

5. Ibid., p. 249.

6. Ibid., p. 250.

7. Ibid., pp. 193–194, 200, 205.

8. See Shirley S. Garrett, "Sisters All," and Deborah Gaitskell, "Housewives, Maids, or Mothers." (References to works listed in the annotated bibliography are by author and short title only.)

9. Ann Miriam Gallagher, "The Indian Nuns," and Asunción Lavrin, "Values and Meaning of Monastic Life."

10. Mary Aquina Weinrich, "A Sociological Study" and "Religious Life in Rhodesia"; "Religious Life for Women in Zaire"; Ancilla Kupalo, "African Sisters' Congregations."

11. See Helen Callaway, "Women in Yoruba Tradition."

12. Charles W. Forman, "Sing to the Lord a New Song." Mercy Amba Odwyoye suggests that in Nigeria the low priority Wesleyan missionaries placed on women's education postponed progress in this regard considerably. See "Standing on Both Feet."

13. T. Omas Ihromi shows variations among different ethnic cultures just within Indonesia itself: "Social and Cultural Background."

14. Cornelia B. Flora, "Pentecostal Women in Colombia"; Ellen Purdy Webster, "Religiosity of Punjabi Christian Girls"; Filomina Chioma Steady, "Protestant Women's Associations."

15. Deborah Gaitskell, "Christian Compounds of Girls," and Bennetta Jules-Rosette, "Women's Initiation in Southern Africa."

16. Kristin Mann, "The Dangers of Dependence," and Barbara Yates, "Church, State, and Education."

1. Images of Chinese Women: Shirley S. Garrett

1. Ida Pruitt, *A Daughter of Han* (Yale University Press, 1945), p. 2.

2. Helen Barrett Montgomery, *Western Women in Eastern Lands* (Macmillan Co., 1910), p. 48.

3. Jennie Hughes, *Chinese Heartthrobs* (Fleming H. Revell Co., 1920), p. 83.

4.. Dame Adelaide Anderson, *Humanity and Labour in China* (London: Student Christian Movement, 1928), p. 164.

5. Pruitt, op. cit., p. 27.

6. Ibid., p. 85.

7. William Edwin Hoy to A. R. Bartholomew, March 11, 1909, "China Mission Minutes," Evangelical and Reformed Church. ("China Mission Minutes" are in Lancaster Theological Seminary, Lancaster, Pa.)

8. F. L. Hawks Pott, *The Emergency in China* (Missionary Education Movement of the United States and Canada, 1913), p. 125.

9. For a good discussion see Yi-tsi Feuerwerker, "Women as Writers in the 1920s and 1930s," in *Women in Chinese Society,* ed. by Margery Wolf and Roxane Witke (Stanford University Press, 1975).

10. For a discussion see Montgomery, op. cit., entire book.

11. Tseng Pao-swen in *Women and the Way,* a symposium (Friendship Press, 1938), p. 33.

12. Montgomery, op. cit., p. 94.

13. Pearl Buck, "Chinese Women," in *Pacific Affairs,* 1931, pp. 904–909.

14. Montgomery, op. cit., pp. 68 et seq.

15. Hughes, op. cit., p. 85.

16. Hawks Pott, op. cit., p. 227.

17. Margaret Burton, *The Education of Women in China* (Fleming H. Revell Co., 1911), p. 90.

18. Tseng, op. cit., p. 29.

19. Margaret Burton, *Notable Women of Modern China* (Fleming H. Revell Co., 1912), p. 107.

20. *Chinese Recorder* (American Presbyterian and Mission Press, Shanghai), June 1890, cited in Burton, *Education of Women,* p. 198.

21. Snyder report in "China Mission Minutes," 1905–1907.

22. Mary Hoy, "China Mission Minutes," Nov. 9, 1902, and Aug. 21, 1921.

23. Yi-tsi Feuerwerker, "In Quest of the Writer Ding Ling," in *Feminist Studies,* vol. 10, no. 1 (Spring 1984), p. 70.

24. Mary Ninde Gamewell, *New Life Currents in China* (Missionary Education Movement, 1919), p. 184.

25. Hawks Pott, op. cit., pp. 126, 139.

26. Ibid., p. 126.
27. Burton, *Education of Women,* p. 188.
28. Gertrude Hoy, "China Mission Minutes," Aug. 15, 1917.
29. Nora Waln, *The House of Exile* (Little, Brown & Co., 1933), pp. 203, 195.
30. Feuerwerker, "Women as Writers."
31. *Chinese Recorder,* vol. 56 (June 1925), p. 348.
32. Edith Pye in *The Asiatic Review,* vol. 25 (April 1929), p. 214.
33. Tseng, op. cit., p. 34.

2. Assumptions About the Indian Woman
Underlying Protestant Church Policies and Programs,
1947–1982: John C. B. Webster

1. The first and third views are quite common. The second may be found in Vina Mazumdar, "The Social Reform Movement in India—From Ranade to Nehru," in *Indian Women: From Purdah to Modernity,* ed. by B. R. Nanda (New Delhi: Vikas Publishing House, 1976), pp. 41–66.

2. The two most prominent were the Women's Indian Association and the All-India Women's Conference founded in 1917 and 1927, respectively.

3. Alice B. Van Doren, "The Women of India," in *The Christian Task in India,* ed. by John McKenzie (London: Macmillan & Co., 1929), pp. 43–65. For earlier views see the reports of the decennial missionary conferences held at Allahabad (1873), Calcutta (1883), Bombay (1893), and Madras (1902).

4. I have relied on the following studies in my analysis of the three stages of the Indian women's movement: Kamaladevi Chattopadhyay, "The Women's Movement—Then and Now," in *Indian Women,* ed. by Devaki Jain (New Delhi: Government of India, 1975), pp. 27–36; Aparna Basu, "The Role of Women in the Indian Struggle for Freedom," in Nanda, ed., op. cit., Note 1, pp. 16–40; Shahida Lateef, "Whither the Indian Women's Movement?" *Economic and Political Weekly,* November 19, 1977, pp. 1948–1951; Vijay Agnew, *Elite Women in Indian Politics* (New Delhi: Vikas Publishing House, 1979); Jana Matson Everett, *Women and Social Change in India* (New Delhi: Heritage, 1979); Shahida Lateef, "The Indian Women's Movement and National Development: An Overview," in *The Extended Family: Women and Political Participation in India and Pakistan,* ed. by Gail Minault (Delhi: Chanakya Publications, 1981), pp. 195–216; Geraldine Forbes, "The Indian Women's Movement: A Struggle for Women's Rights or National Liberation?" in Minault, ed., op. cit., pp. 49–82.

5. V. V. Ujagare, "Christian Marriage Laws in India—A Case for Reforms," *National Christian Council Review* (hereafter referred to as *NCCR*), May 1974, p. 273.

6. E. D. Devadasan, "Laws of Succession Applicable to Christians in India," *NCCR,* June–July 1972, pp. 252–259.

7. Kaj Baago, *A History of the National Christian Council of India 1914–1964* (Nagpur: National Christian Council, 1965), p. 77.

8. *The Ministry of Women* is referred to in "Editorials: The Ministry of Women," *NCCR,* April 1962, p. 142, but I have not been able to see the report itself.

9. L. W. Bryce and Elizabeth Moreland, *The Life and Work of Women in the Church in India and Pakistan* (n.d.), pp. 19, 25, and 44.

10. Ibid., pp. 36–37.

11. Ibid., pp. 73–74.

12. M. H. Wigam, "Educated Christian Women and the Missionary Vocation," *NCCR,* October 1948, pp. 408–413.

13. Ibid.; also E. L. Ananta Rao, "The Spiritual Growth of the Rural Churches," *NCCR,* October 1947, p. 487, and Carol Graham, "Women in the Indian Church" *Indian Journal of Theology,* VII (Oct.–Dec. 1958), pp. 145–151. In 1962 Carol Graham wrote that "the women are not prepared to offer themselves because they do not see anything worth doing that the Church is prepared to offer them and the Church is not inclined to positive action until the women are actually there. Consequently the women continue to fail the Church and the Church to fail the women. Somewhere there must be a breakthrough and it seems as if it must come from the side of the Church" ("Theological Education for Women," *NCCR,* August 1962, p. 277).

14. Shashi Sail, "Women—Subjects of Their Own Destiny," *NCCR,* October 1979, pp. 503–509.

15. Mrs. K. K. George, "Editorial: International Women's Year," *NCCR,* August 1975, pp. 348–351; Elizabeth George, "Is Equality the Goal of Women's Liberation?" ibid., pp. 360–363.

16. "International Women's Year 1975," *NCCR,* April 1975, pp. 203–206; Shanti Solomon, "Christian Women in Witness and Service," *NCCR,* January 1977, pp. 37–41; E. Anchees, "The Role of Christian Women's Organizations in the Context of the Struggle for Justice," *NCCR,* May 1979, pp. 271–278; Sail, loc. cit., Note 14.

17. Mrs. K. K. George, loc. cit., Note 15; Elizabeth George, loc. cit., Note 15; Mathai Zachariah, "Editorial: Women's Search for a Fuller Humanity," *NCCR,* October 1976, pp. 500–503.

18. Leelamma Athyal, "Women and Service—A Theological Perspective," *NCCR,* May 1981, pp. 262–275. These had been common themes at the World Council of Churches' Asian Consultation on "The Community of Women and Men in the Church" held at Bangalore in August 1978, in which most of the participants were Indian Protestants.

19. The Protestant body that has probably gone farthest in acting on this premise is the Joint Women's Programme of the Christian Institute for the Study of Religion and Society and William Carey Study and Research Center. It is described in "The JWP," *Banhi,* July 1980, p. 1.

20. Bengt Sundkler, *Church of South India: The Movement Towards Union, 1900–1947* (London: Lutterworth Press, 1954); Marcus Ward, *The Pilgrim Church: An Account of the First Five Years in the Life of the Church of South India* (London: Epworth Press, 1953).

21. Carol Graham, "News and Notes: Women's Work Leaders Conference," *South India Churchman* (hereafter referred to as *SIC*), March 1948, p. 111.

22. Minutes of the Women's Fellowship Central Executive, Sept. 2–3, 1958.

23. "Ye Are Now the People of God" in 1963, "Thy Kingdom Come" in 1966, and "Who Is My Neighbour?" in 1970.

24. The fourth objective had become the first one, while the wording of the third was changed from "truly Christian home life" to "truly Christian life" and placed second. Women's Fellowship of the Church of South India, *Hand Book* (4th ed., 1969), p. 1.

25. "From Our Diocesan Correspondents: Dornakal," *SIC*, October 1949, p. 195; Carol Graham, "Co-operation Between Men and Women in Church and Society," *SIC*, December 1955, pp. 5–6; Carol Graham, "The Cooperation of Men and Women in the Church," *SIC*, July 1959, pp. 6 and 16; Margaret Harris, "Women's Column: Partnership of Men and Women in the Church," *SIC*, November 1964, pp. 3–4.

26. The pastor's wife was normally to be president of the pastorate women's fellowship and the bishop's wife was normally to be president of the diocesan women's fellowship. *Hand Book*, Note 24, pp. 10–11.

27. Minutes of the Women's Fellowship Central Executive, Sept. 6–8, 1957, and Minutes of the CSI Women's Fellowship Central Committee, August 28–30, 1964.

28. Women's Fellowship of the Church of South India, *Hand Book* (5th ed., 1980), p. 1.

29. *The Order for Women in the Church of South India* (1963), p. 1.

30. *The Synod of the Church of South India. Third Statutory Session. January 12th to 16th, 1952—Masulipatam,* p. 85; Rajaiah D. Paul, *Ecumenism in Action* (Madras: Christian Literature Society, 1972), p. 299. (Hereafter the Proceedings of the Synod of the Church of South India will be referred to as *CSISP* with the year added, e.g., *CSISP, 1952.*)

31. *The Constitution of the Church of South India* (1972), p. 57.

32. *CSISP, 1970,* p. 130.

33. Ibid., pp. 35 and 41.

34. *CSISP, 1972,* p. 30.

35. "C.S.I. Synod Theological Commission," *SIC,* November 1975, p. 6.

36. Ibid., p. 7.

37. *CSISP, 1976,* p. 28.

38. *CSISP, 1978,* pp. 19–20.

39. *CSISP, 1980,* p. 24.

40. *CSISP, 1982,* p. 23.

41. *CSISP, 1976,* p. 21.

42. *CSISP, 1978,* p. 12.

43. *CSISP, 1980,* p. 37.

44. *CSISP, 1982,* p. 27.

45. Sister Betty Paul, "Women and Church Administration," *SIC,* October 1973, pp. 11–12.

46. Clara Clarke, "Women in the Life of the C.S.I.," *SIC*, Jubilee Number 1972, p. 48.

47. Daisy Gopal Ratnam, "Status of Indian Women in Their Country and in the Church," *SIC*, July 1975, pp. 2–3.

48. "Church of South India. A Report of the Consultation on Priorities for the Mission of the Church—September 24–October 1, 1981," *SIC*, December 1981, pp. 3–5.

49. Dena Ratnam, "The Working Wife and Mother," *SIC*, May 1969, p. 8; Saro Sundersingh, "The Christian Faith and the Housewife," *SIC*, September 1970, pp. 7–8; Sister Grace Aaron, "Pastoral Ministry Among Women," *SIC*, March 1971, p. 6.

50. D. L. Gopal Ratnam, "Challenge to the Members of the Women's Fellowship," *SIC*, December 1974, pp. 3–4; Mrs. S. T. Cornelius, "The Church and International Women's Year," *SIC*, September 1975, pp. 8–9; "Role of Women in CSI—An Evaluation," *SIC*, September 1979, p. 4.

51. Supporters of the status quo, especially at the popular level, seem more prone to use psychological stereotypes (e.g., woman as weak, shy, and dependent by nature) and to use the liberated Western woman as a negative example of what the Indian woman would inevitably become if change were to occur. See the appendix on "Women in Some Bangalore Churches, 1980 and 1983" in John C. B. Webster and Ellen Low Webster, "Teaching Indian Seminarians About the Church and Women," in *The Emerging Christian Woman: Church and Society Perspectives*, ed. by S. Faria, A. Alexander, and J. B. Tellis-Nayak (Indore: Satprakashan Sanchar Kendra, 1984), pp. 257–260.

52. This mode of thinking is made quite explicit in Manisha Roy, "The Concepts of 'Femininity' and 'Liberation' in the Context of Changing Sex-Roles: Women in Modern India and America," in *Being Female: Reproduction, Power and Change*, ed. by Dana Raphael (The Hague: Mouton Publishers, 1975), pp. 219–230. It is also built into the framework of inquiry of most other studies of Indian women.

53. Patricia Caplan, "Women's Organizations in Madras City, India," in *Women United, Women Divided: Comparative Studies of Ten Contemporary Cultures*, ed. by Patricia Caplan and Janet M. Bujra (Indiana University Press, 1979), p. 123. See also Gail Minault, "Introduction: The Extended Family as Metaphor and the Expansion of Women's Realm," in Minault, ed., op. cit., Note 45, pp. 3–18.

54. George Kurian and Mariam John, "Women and Social Customs Within the Family: A Case Study of Attitudes in Kerala, India," in Raphael, ed., op. cit., Note 52, pp. 255–265; N. S. Krishnakumari and A. S. Geetha, *A Report on the Problem of Dowry in Bangalore City* (Calcutta: Joint Women's Programme, 1983); *Towards Equality: Report of the Committee on the Status of Women in India* (New Delhi: Government of India, 1974), pp. 393–453.

55. Daisy Gopal Ratnam, loc. cit., Note 47.

56. *Good News for Women*, ed. by Jyotsna Chatterji (Delhi: I.S.P.C.K., 1979 and 1981). She then edited a second in this series entitled *Women in Praise and Struggle* (Delhi: I.S.P.C.K., 1982).

3. Sor Juana Inés de la Cruz: Beatriz Melano Couch

1. See, for example, the prologue and notes in Spanish by Alfonso Méndez Plancarte in *Obras Completas de Sor Juana Inés de la Cruz* (Mexico: Fondo de Cultura Económica, 1951–1957).

2. Ibid., vol. 4: *Respuesta a Sor Filotea de la Cruz.*

3. Ibid.

4. Ibid.

5. Ibid.

6. Ibid.

7. Ramón Xirau, *Genio y figura de Sor Juana Inés de la Cruz* (Buenos Aires: Eudeba, 1967), p. 158.

8. *Obras Completas,* vol. 4, p. 617.

9. Xirau, op. cit., p. 169.

10. Is she not clearly going beyond Augustine's theology in the affirmation that the human being is completely restored through Christ's death to what Paul calls the "new man in Christ"? There is no mention here of original sin, which is Augustine's explanation of the fact of the presence of evil in the world and in the human being, even after Christ's death and resurrection.

11. Sor Juana shows in brief passages, where she reflects theologically on the sacrament, an impressive degree of freedom and creativity. Although she never specifically rejects classic Roman Catholic sacramental theology in those of her writings that have survived, it seems characteristic of her to approach the sacrament from other angles. Although there are good reasons for concluding that Reformation theology did not have a formative influence on her, there are parts of her thought here that make us seriously wonder if her way of thinking was not in some unknown way enriched by some Reformed thinker(s). If this is not the case, her innovations are all the more striking.

12. Xirau, op. cit., pp. 83–84.

13. *Obras Completas,* vol. 4; Xirau, op. cit., pp. 26–66.

14. "It is the best philosophical poem in the Spanish language": Xirau, op. cit., p. 85.

15. Cf. "Sueño de un sueño," *Historia Mexicana* (El Colegio de Mexico), vol. 10, p. 1.

4. Coming of Age in a Latin Church: Katherine Gilfeather, M.M.

1. Margaret Mead, *Coming of Age in Samoa* (William Morrow & Co., 1974), p. 3.

2. *Pastoral Plan of the Chilean Episcopate, 1961–1962* (Santiago: Centro Bellarmino, 1962).

3. Katherine Gilfeather, *Las Religiosas y el Mundo en Cambio* (Santiago: Centro Bellarmino, 1970).

4. Brian H. Smith, *The Church and Politics in Chile* (Princeton University Press, 1982), pp. 48, 344.

5. Galilea, Katherine Gilfeather, and Puga, *Las Mujeres que Trabajan en la Iglesia—La Experiencia Chilena* (Santiago: Centro Bellarmino, 1976).

6. See Note 2, above.

7. "Poverty in the Church," *Second General Conference of Latin American Bishops* (Bogotá: General Secretariat of CELAM, 1969).

8. Ibid.

9. Kenneth A. Briggs, "Women and the Church," *The New York Times Magazine,* November 6, 1983, p. 126.

10. Katherine Gilfeather, *Perfil Actual de la Candidata a la Vida Religiosa Chilena* (Santiago: Centro Bellarmino, 1983).

11. Maria Rainer Rilke, *Letters to a Young Poet,* trans. M. D. Herter (W. W. Norton & Co., 1954), pp. 64–65.

5. Catholic Women of India: Stella Faria

1. "Decree on the Apostolate of the Laity," *The Documents of Vatican II* (Guild Press, 1966), p. 500.

2. *The New Leader,* February 19, 1984, p. 1.

3. The CBCI, which was constituted at the Metropolitans' Conference held in Madras in September 1944, is a permanent association of the Catholic hierarchy of India.

4. Statement issued at the first National Convention of Lay Leaders held under the auspices of the Laity Commission of the CBCI in Mangalore, December 1983.

5. Ibid.

6. *The Examiner,* March 10, 1984, p. 146.

7. Ibid.

8. *Catholic India* (New Delhi: CBCI Centre, 1982). This special brochure, prepared for the Indo-German Bishops Colloquium, Tiruchirapalli, January 15–16, 1982, is not paginated.

9. Ibid.

10. Ibid.

11. Ibid.

12. Ibid.

13. "Decree on the Appropriate Renewal of the Religious Life," *Vatican Council II: The Conciliar and Post Conciliar Documents* (Bombay: St. Paul's Publications, 1975), p. 554.

14. Cecilia Arokiaswamy, "Women Religious and Their Ministries to Other Women." This unpublished article is not paginated.

15. Engelbert Zeitler, "The Dawn of a New Age for Women in the Indian Church," in *Women in India and in the Church,* ed. by Engelbert Zeitler et al. (Pune: Ishvani Kendra, 1978), p. 193.

16. "Final Statement," in *The Indian Church in the Struggle for a New Society,* ed. by D. S. Amalorpavadass (Bangalore: National Biblical, Catechetical, and Liturgical Centre, 1981), p. 72.

17. M. Carol, "Women Religious and the New Society," in *The Emerging Christian Woman: Church and Society Perspectives,* ed. by Stella Faria et al. (Indore: Satprakashan Sanchar Kendra, 1984), p. 211.

18. Ibid.

19. "Aspiration of a Just Society," *Report of the Annual General Meeting of the CRI,* Women Section (Bangalore: National Biblical, Catechetical, and Liturgical Centre, 1973), p. 39.

20. *Neythri,* February 19, 1984, p. 2.

21. CCWI Annual Report, 1974.

22. Stella Faria, Anna V. Alexander, and Jessie B. Tellis-Nayak, eds., *The Emerging Christian Woman: Church and Society Perspectives* (Indore: Satprakashan Sanchar Kendra, 1984).

6. The Role of Women in Africa's New Religions: Bennetta Jules-Rosette

1. These figures are taken from *World Christian Encyclopedia: A Comparative Study of Churches in the Modern World, A.D. 1900–2000,* ed. by David B. Barrett (Oxford University Press, 1982), pp. 782 and 791. This collection contains an overview of Christian churches and new religions on a worldwide scale and an update of the editor's previous statistical estimates on the growth of new African religious movements.

2. Wyatt MacGaffey points out that Portuguese missionaries first brought Christianity to the Kongo Kingdom during the fifteenth century. See *Modern Kongo Prophets: Religion in a Plural Society* (Indiana University Press, 1983), pp. 25–30. These prophetic movements preceded the contemporary religious groups discussed at more length in this article. Following Jacob Needleman in *The New Religions* (Doubleday, 1970) and *The New Religious Consciousness,* ed. by Charles Glock and Robert Bellah (University of California Press, 1976), I have referred to the contemporary African movements as "new religions." These African movements actually cover a much broader time period than the U.S. new religions, which are dated as covering the past twenty years. The new African movements date back to the 1920s and have appeared since then in various forms. See also Bryan Wilson, *Religion in Sociological Perspective* (Oxford University Press, 1982), pp. 142–147, for a comparison between U.S. and African new religions.

3. I have analyzed the role of women in African churches in the following: "Women as Ceremonial Leaders in an African Church: The Apostles of John Maranke," in *The New Religions of Africa* (Ablex Publishing Corp., 1979), pp. 127–144, and "Women in Indigenous African Cults and Churches," in *The Black Woman Cross-Culturally,* ed. by Filomina Chioma Steady (Schenkman Publishing Corp., 1981), pp. 185–207.

4. Several sources present accounts of the early prophetic movements in the Kongo Kingdom of San Salvador. These accounts emphasize the similarities between the Antonians (followers of Dona Béatrice) and contemporary African indigenous churches. Sources include Jan Vansina, *Kingdoms of the Savanna* (University of Wisconsin Press, 1968), p. 154: André Doutreloux, "Prophétisme et Culture," in *African Systems of Thought,* ed. by Meyer Fortes and Germaine Dieterlin (International African Institute, 1965); Efraim Andersson, *Messianic Popular Movements in the Lower Congo* (Uppsala: (Almquist and Wiksells, 1958), pp. 244–255; and MacGaffey, op. cit., pp. 26–50. Similarly, women in

leadership positions in medieval Christianity in Europe were more often associated with heretical movements.

5. These descriptions are suggested by Andersson, op. cit., p. 244.

6. See Carol P. Hoffer, "Madam Yoko: Ruler of the Kpa Mende Confederacy," in *Women, Culture, and Society*, ed. by Michelle Zimbalist Rosaldo and Louise Lamphere (Stanford University Press, 1974), pp. 173–187.

7. William Wade Harris, a Grebo from Liberia, converted large numbers of people in the Ivory Coast, Ghana, and Liberia in 1913 and 1914. See Sheila S. Walker, *The Religious Revolution in the Ivory Coast: The Prophet Harris and the Harrist Church* (University of North Carolina Press, 1983), pp. 35–55. Subsequently, a number of Harris's converts established offshoot movements espousing the original founder's doctrines. These groups include the Déima cult described here. The practices of some of these offshoot movements were combined with traditional religious rituals, especially in the rural area. The Déima movement has been described briefly in the following: Denise Paulme, "Une Religion Syncretique en Côte d'Ivoire: Le Culte Déima," *Cahiers d'Études Africaines*, vol. 1 (1962), pp. 5–90; Sheila S. Walker, "Women in the Harrist Movement," in Jules-Rosette, *The New Religions of Africa*, pp. 87–97.

8. Marie-Louise Martin, "The Mai Chaza Church in Rhodesia," in *African Initiatives in Religion*, ed. by David B. Barrett (Nairobi, Kenya: East African Publishing House, 1971), p. 111. Martin discusses Mai Chaza's rejection of a feminine identity as a feature of her ability to assume leadership.

9. Little has been published on Mai Chaza's movement. The most definitive account is probably the brief essay by Marie-Louise Martin describing the origins, ritual, and social organization of the group. See "The Mai Chaza Church in Rhodesia," pp. 109–121.

10. In 1974 I analyzed the direction that Lenshina's movement appeared to be taking in the early 1970s. My predictions concerning Lenshina's inability to pass on leadership to a woman successor have since proven to be the case. See Bennetta Jules-Rosette, "Ceremony and Leadership: The Influence of Women in African Independent Churches," paper presented at the UCLA African Studies Center Colloquium "Women and Change in Africa, 1870–1970," Los Angeles, April 1974. See also John V. Taylor and Dorothea A. Lehmann, *Christians of the Copperbelt* (London: SCM Press, 1961), pp. 248–268, for a discussion of the early years of the Lenshina movement.

11. Both Sister Mary Aquina and Marie-France Perrin Jassy argue that positions of ceremonial leadership for women may ultimately imply political subordination rather than increasing access to positions of political power. Mary Aquina, "The People of the Spirit: An Independent Church in Rhodesia," *Africa* (London) 37 (1967):206; Marie-France Perrin Jassy, "Women in the African Independent Churches," *Risk* 7 (1971):46–49.

12. This group has been analyzed in the context of local communities and everyday religious practices appearing in the new religious movements among the Luo of Tanzania. Cf. Marie-France Perrin Jassy, *La Communauté de Base dans les Églises Africaines*, Centre des Études Ethnologiques, série 2, vol. 3 (Bandundu, Zaire, 1970), pp. 80–82.

13. Carol P. MacCormack describes the ritual separation and complementarity that are part of the Sande secret society of Sierra Leone. In the Sande organization, women control their own initiation rites and share political control over the village with men. See Carol P. MacCormack, "Sande: The Public Face of a Secret Society," in Jules-Rosette, *The New Religions of Africa,* pp. 27–37. The Sande society also plays important roles in marriage and kinship arrangements, midwifery, healing, and personal counseling for its members. See Denise Lardner Carmody, *Women and World Religions* (Parthenon Press, 1979), pp. 33–36.

14. Bengt G. M. Sundkler, *Zulu Zion and Some Swazi Zionists* (London: Oxford University Press, 1976), pp. 30–31.

15. Geoffrey Parrinder, *Religion in Africa* (Harmondsworth, England: Penguin Books, 1969), p. 159.

16. This quote is taken from Bryan R. Wilson, *Magic and the Millennium: A Sociological Study of Religious Movements of Protest Among Tribal and Third World Peoples* (Harper & Row, 1973), p. 348.

17. Rita Gross, "Methodological Remarks on the Study of Women in Religion: Review, Criticism and Redefinition," in *Women and Religion,* ed. by Judith Plaskow and Joan Arnold Romero (Scholars Press, 1974), p. 153.

18. Bennetta Jules-Rosette, *African Apostles* (Cornell University Press, 1975), pp. 43–44.

19. J.D.Y. Peel, *Aladura: A Religious Movement Among the Yoruba* (London: International African Institute, 1968), pp. 169–170.

20. See Carmody, op. cit., pp. 125–126, and Penelope G. Washbourn, "Differentiation and Difference: Reflections on the Ethical Implications of Women's Liberation," in *Women and Religion,* pp. 129–136. Both authors emphasize the importance of the "virginity myth" as a source of religious symbolism for women in the Judeo-Christian tradition.

21. These young women were given to John Masowe by their families at an early age. Eventually, some of these women were allowed to marry other church elders with John Masowe's approval. Cf. Clive Dillon-Malone, *Korsten Basketmakers* (Institute for African Studies, 1978), pp. 62–63, and Marthinus L. Daneel, *Old and New in Southern Shona Independent Churches,* vol. 1: *Background and Rise of the Major Movements* (The Hague: Mouton, 1971), pp. 339–349.

22. See Janice Raymond, "Beyond Male Morality," in *Women and Religion,* pp. 115–125.

23. I. M. Lewis is concerned with gender distinctions in imagery and symbolism in ecstatic religion. He describes the effects of such imagery in various religious cults. See I. M. Lewis, *Ecstatic Religion: An Anthropological Study of Spirit Possession and Shamanism* (Middlesex, England: Penguin Books, 1971), pp. 58–59.

24. Jules-Rosette, *African Apostles,* p. 66.

25. In my book *Symbols of Change: Urban Transition in a Zambian Community* (Ablex Publishing Corp., 1981) I discuss the role of women's domestic groups among the Maranke and Masowe apostles as reinforcing a sense of commitment to and identification with the group. Particularly within polygynous families, such identification appears to be strengthened within the household

unit. Thus the household unit itself constitutes a religious associational sub-grouping for these women.

26. Ilsa Schuster discusses the roles of first-generation migrant women and their urban daughters in Lusaka, Zambia, with regard to changing religious beliefs. These women adapt folk and Christian religious beliefs to meet the needs of their socioeconomic settings. See Ilsa Schuster, *New Women of Lusaka* (Mayfield Publishing Co., 1979), pp. 30–40.

27. Elsewhere, I have noted the fact that new forms of women's initiation rites seem to be increasing in the urban areas of southern Africa. These rites include combined ceremonies performed together by members of diverse ethnic groups (e.g., the Bemba, Ngoni, and Cewa women in Lusaka, Zambia) as well as modified forms of initiation incorporated into the ceremonies of Africa's indigenous churches. In both cases these initiation rites appear to focus on the household skills and domestic roles of women in the city. These ceremonies involve a form of cultural substitution that symbolically recalls but does not entirely supplant the customary rites. Bennetta Jules-Rosette, "Changing Aspects of Women's Initiation in Southern Africa," *Canadian Journal of African Studies* 13 (1980):1–16.

28. Judith Van Allen describes the economic associations developed by West African market women. Such groups have a direct impact on the economic lives of urban women. See "Women in Africa: Modernization Means More Dependency," *Center Magazine* (Center for the Study of Democratic Institutions), May/June 1974, pp. 60–67.

29. Barbara C. Lewis has described the growth of women's marketeers' associations in West Africa in "The Limitations of Group Action Among Entrepreneurs: The Market Women of Abidjan, Ivory Coast," in *Women in Africa*, ed. by Nancy J. Hafkin and Edna G. Bay (Stanford University Press, 1976), pp. 135–156. Her materials and my own research in urban Zambia suggest that religious and work associations do *not* tend to overlap in the city. Although cottage industries have formed within the indigenous churches in Lusaka, Zambia, these enterprises involve men in work associations on a much larger scale than they do women.

30. Elsewhere, I have referred to this utopian reality as the arcadian wish for the return to a simpler but transformed way of life in which role definitions for men and women are modified through religious ceremony: *New Religions of Africa*, pp. 219–229.

7. Third World Women and Men: Constance F. Parvey

1. The Asian Consultation on the Community of Women and Men in the Church, Bangalore, India, 1978.

2. See Betty Thompson, *A Chance to Change* (Fortress Press, 1982), and Constance F. Parvey, *The Community of Women and Men in the Church* (Fortress Press, 1983).

3. The six regional reports are *Report of the Regional Consultation on the Community of Men and Women in the Church Study* (Nairobi: An All-African

Conference of Churches Production, 1981); *The Community of Women and Men in the Church: Report of the Asian Consultation* (Bangalore, India, 1978); *A Space to Grow In: European Regional Consultation, Community of Women and Men in the Church Study* (Geneva: World Council of Churches, Commission on Faith and Order, CWMC, 1980); *Latin American Consultation: The Community of Women and Men in the Church* (Geneva: World Council of Churches, Commission on Faith and Order, CWMC, 1981; also published in Spanish by the Seminario Bíblico Latinoamericano [San José, Costa Rica], 1981); *Middle East Council of Churches Consultation: The Community of Women and Men in the Church* (Geneva: World Council of Churches and the Middle East Council of Churches, 1980); and *Community of Women and Men in the Church: A Gathering to Share Our Hope* (National Council of Churches, Commission on Faith and Order, 1980). Other related documents are "Authority and Community in Christian Tradition," drafted by Madeleine Boucher, and "Women and Unity: Problem or Possibility," by Letty Russell. These were also published by the NCC's Faith and Order Commission.

4. High-caste families with property to preserve gave dowries, whereas low-caste families paid a price for the bride because she was an added worker in the groom's family.

5. *The Community of Women and Men in the Church: Report of the Asian Consultation,* p. 40.

6. Ibid., p. 38.

7. Ibid.

8. Ibid., pp. 73–74.

9. Ibid., p. v.

10. Ibid., p. 17.

11. Ibid., p. 33.

12. Ibid., p. 85.

13. Ibid., p. 99.

14. *Report of the Regional Consultation on Community of Men and Women in the Church, Nairobi,* p. 26.

15. Ibid., p. 29.

16. Ibid., p. iii.

17. Ibid., p. 31.

18. Ibid.

19. Ibid.

20. Ibid., p. 34.

21. Ibid., p. 49.

22. Ibid., p. 34.

23. Ibid., p. 27.

24. Ibid.

25. Ibid., p. 35.

26. Ibid.

27. Ibid., p. 37.

28. Ibid.

29. Ibid., p. 24.

30. Ibid., p. 45.

31. Ibid., pp. 59–60.
32. Ibid., pp. 58–59.

8. Women in Philippine Basic Christian Communities:
Mark Jeffery Ratkus

1. The Spanish phrase *comunidades eclesiales de base* is rendered in the Philippines as Basic, rather than as Base, Christian Communities.

2. This chapter could not have been written without the valuable insights of Sister Aloysia Albert, C.M., and Fathers Romeo Empestan and Rufino Suplido; my thanks go to them. To Father Brian Gore, S.S.C., I owe my deepest gratitude for having me accompany him and his pastoral team visiting the BCCs (October 18–29, 1980) and for helping me to interpret the overwhelmingly inspirational experiences I had among these simple hill folk.

3. Pope John XXIII, *Peace on Earth (Pacem in Terris)* in *Seven Great Encyclicals*, ed. by William J. Gibbons, S.J. (Paulist Press, 1963), p. 320.

4. Vatican II, *Pastoral Constitution on the Church in the Modern World (Gaudium et Spes)* (National Catholic Welfare Conference, 1965), p. 25.

5. Pope Paul VI, *On the Development of Peoples (Populorum Progressio)* (United States Catholic Conference, 1967), p. 7.

6. Synod of Bishops, Rome, 1971, *Justice in the World* (National Conference of Catholic Bishops, 1972), pp. 33–34.

7. "The Difference Between Dissent and Subversion," *Origins: NC Documentary Service*, vol. 12, no. 39 (March 18, 1983), p. 619.

8. *The Philippines: Human Settlements* (National Media Production Center [Manila], 1979), pp. 4–5; David Joel Steinberg, *The Philippines: A Singular and a Plural Place* (Westview Press, 1982), pp. 114–115.

9. "The Chains of Injustice," *Columban Mission*, vol. 66, no. 1 (January 1983), p. 4.

10. "Man with a Mission: Fr. Niall O'Brien," *Columban Mission*, vol. 66, no. 1 (January 1983), p. 8.

11. "Chains of Injustice," loc. cit.

12. "Parish Profiles: Oringao Parish," *Jubilee News: Newsletter for the Golden Jubilee Celebration of the Diocese of Bacolod*, no. 5 (October 1982), p. 4.

13. Steinberg, op. cit., p. 73.

14. "Report from Kabankalan (insert)," *Columban Mission*, vol. 66, no. 8 (October 1983), pp. 2–4.

15. Ibid., p. 3.

16. *The Philippines: Human Settlements*, op. cit. Note 8, p. 1.

17. Ibid.

18. E. S. Browning, "Philippine Communists Make Inroads," *Wall Street Journal*, July 12, 1983, p. 43.

19. Lorna Kalaw-Tirol, "In This Catholic Country, Is It Subversive to Live Out Christ's Gospel?" *Philippine Panorama*, November 21, 1982, pp. 5–6.

20. Sister Aloysia Albert, C.M., letter of August 23, 1983, in response to a questionnaire composed by author.

21. Christine P. Eleazar, Isabel Rojas-Aleta, and Teresita L. Silva, *A Profile of Filipino Women: Their Status and Role* (Manila: Philippine Business for Social Progress, 1977), p. 195.

22. Lourdes R. Quisumbing, "The Filipino Family and Philippine Society in the 80's," *Asian Thought & Society,* vol. 7, no. 19 (March 1982), p. 37.

23. Clark D. Neher, "Sex Roles in the Philippines: The Ambiguous Cebuana," in *Women of Southeast Asia,* ed. by Penny Van Esterik, Occasional Paper No. 9 of the "Monograph Series on Southeast Asia" (Northern Illinois University, Center for Southeast Asian Studies, 1982), pp. 156, 158.

24. Quisumbing, loc. cit., p. 35.

25. Neher, loc. cit., pp. 159–160.

26. Nancy Folbre, "Household Production in the Philippines: A Non-Neoclassical Approach," Working Paper #26 of the Michigan State University Office of Women in International Development, June 1983, p. 8.

27. Ibid., p. 9; Robert Orr Whyte and Pauline Whyte, *The Women of Rural Asia* (Westview Press, 1982), p. 150.

28. Eleazar et al., op. cit., p. 202.

29. Ibid., p. 203; Neher, loc. cit., pp. 171–173.

30. Quisumbing, loc. cit., pp. 34, 36; Eleazar et al., op. cit., p. 208.

31. M. Christina Szanton, "Women and Men in Iloilo, Philippines: 1903–1970," in Van Esterik (loc. cit. Note 23), pp. 134–135.

32. Whyte and Whyte, op. cit., p. 150.

33. Szanton, loc. cit., pp. 132, 144–145.

34. Eleazar et al., op. cit., p. 304.

35. Ibid., pp. 209–210.

36. Ibid., p. 303.

37. Ibid., p. 209.

38. Ibid., pp. 204–205.

39. Teresa J. Ho, "Time Costs of Child Rearing in the Rural Philippines," *Population and Development Review,* vol. 5, no. 4 (1979), pp. 648–649.

40. Folbre, op. cit., p. 12.

41. Eleazar et al., op. cit., p. 303.

42. Ho, loc. cit., pp. 645, 659.

43. Ibid., p. 651.

44. Folbre, op. cit., p. 9.

45. Eleazar et al., op. cit., pp. 201–202.

46. Father Romeo Empestan, letter of September 2, 1983, in response to a questionnaire composed by author.

47. Fr. Rufino Suplido, letter of September 2, 1983, in response to a questionnaire composed by author.

48. Empestan, loc. cit.

49. Ibid.

50. Eleazar et al., op. cit., pp. 210–211.

51. Ibid., pp. 326–327.